D1175536

From the Mango Tree
and Other Folktales
from Nepal

World Folklore Series

Selections Available on Audiocassette

From the Mango Tree and Other Folktales from Nepal

Kavita Ram Shrestha

and

Sarah Lamstein

1997
Libraries Unlimited, Inc.
Englewood, Colorado

To my father—KRS
To Joel—SL

Libraries Unlimited, Inc.
P.O. Box 6633
Englewood, CO 80155-6633
1-800-237-6124

Production Editor: Kevin W. Perizzolo
Copy Editor: Curtis D. Holmes
Proofreader: Eileen Bartlett
Interior Design and Typesetting: Judy Gay Matthews

Library of Congress Cataloging-in-Publication Data

Shrestha, Kavita Ram.
  From the mango tree and other folktales from Nepal / Kavita Ram
Shrestha and Sarah Lamstein.
  x, 120 p. 19x26 cm. (World folklore series)
  Includes bibliographical references.
  ISBN 1-56308-378-7
  1. Tales--Nepal. I. Lamstein, Sarah, 1943-   . II. Title.
III. Series.
GR307.N4S57 1997
398.2'095496--dc20   96-24539
                                                          CIP

Contents

Preface

Our first trip to Nepal was in the summer of 1973, when my husband was working with USAID and the Nepalese Ministry of Health. I was immediately captivated by the country, the gentleness of the people, the spectacular beauty of the land, the aura of exotic spirituality—a most compelling combination. I wanted to share this wonderful place with family and friends in the United States. When I met Kavita Ram Shrestha and learned he was a writer, I knew I had found a way. We decided to collaborate on a folktale project. Kavita selected and translated the tales, and I then reworked them.

In 1981 our family again went to Nepal. Though much was the same as we had remembered—the sights, the smells, the ubiquitous signs of worship—we noticed some dramatic changes, especially in the capital city, Kathmandu. Traffic had increased greatly and the air was much dirtier. And the people were becoming more vocal in their protests against their poor living conditions.

Since our last visit to the country, even more has changed. The king now serves a largely ceremonial function, as the people are grappling with a representative government. Pollution in downtown Kathmandu is almost unbearable, and the distinctive, beautiful brick and carved wooden houses of the valley are being shouted down by new, graceless, concrete structures. The influence of television is pervasive. Though rural life remains little changed, change is inevitable. In light of the rapid political and technological shifts, it is especially comforting to work with the folk literature, passed down and cherished for generations.

The storytelling tradition is strong in Nepal, and Kavita Ram Shrestha, the collector and translator of these tales, is eager to preserve it. As a boy, he listened to several tellers, including his father, Nanda Ram Shrestha, his maternal uncle, Harka Bahadur Shrestha—his favorite storyteller—and his cousin-brother, Narayan Das Shrestha.

The tales that Kavita has collected are primarily of the folk tradition, rather than from the religious or historical traditions. They reflect the poor station of the people, looking upward to the lives of kings and elevating the poor to positions of good fortune. The themes are common to folk literature worldwide, kindness and pluck rewarded, pride and jealousy condemned. The tales in the pourquoi genre explain the origins of certain lakes, caves, and rivers, and why death is both silent and invisible.

This collection of folktales from Nepal is the only one published in the United States that is currently in print. One of the tales, "The Farmer and the Jackal," appeared in the children's magazine *Faces* and has since been published in an anthology for reading teachers, *Reading and Responding*. Adding to the presence of Nepalese literature in the United States, the University of California Press recently published an anthology of contemporary Nepalese poetry and short stories, *Himalayan Voices,* edited by Michael J. Hutt. In addition, there are a number of beautiful photographic studies of the land and culture, as well as entertaining, thoughtful travelogues, gripping accounts of mountaineering expeditions, and some excellent children's books that offer a good overview of the country. Some of these books are noted in the bibliography.

It has been a most satisfying experience collaborating with Kavita Ram Shrestha, both for his enthusiasm and his unerring literary sense. Kavita Ram began writing stories and poems when he was nine years old, and he has been writing ever since. In high school, one of four Ram Bahadurs in his class, his teacher changed his name to Kavita Ram, or "the Ram who writes poems." Kavita Ram credits his father with encouraging him to listen and to write.

I would like to thank my parents and my friends Judith Beth Cohen and Cola Franzen for their consistent guidance and sustenance through the writing life. Deeply felt thanks to John Comings for sharing his photographs taken over many years in Nepal and for his critique of the manuscript. Thanks to John's friend Stephen Frantz for his pictures of the mountains. Thanks also to Chij Shrestha for his quiet wisdom. I am grateful to Larry Benowitz for his photographs of the Everest region and for his conversation, and to Brad Pratt for his cheerful and apt rendering of Nepalese designs.

Heartfelt appreciation to my children Joshua, Emily, and Abigail for their forbearance during the many hours I spent at the computer. I am especially proud to include Emily's photographs, which she took on a recent trip to Nepal. My husband Joel's photos further enliven the album and contribute to the family feeling of this project. Through Joel's work and generosity, he has opened our eyes to the world. For this, I am singularly grateful.

To the people of Nepal, *Namaste!* I salute the spirit within you.

—Sarah Lamstein

Taken from *Let's Go to Nepal,* first published in the United Kingdom by the Watts Publishing Group, 96 Leonard Street, London EC2A 4RH.

An Introduction to Nepal

Overview

Nepal is one of the most beautiful places on earth. One can look out from the Kathmandu Valley over lush green cultivated fields, beyond that, on the tender green of terraced mountain slopes, and in the distance, on the snowcapped peaks of the Himalayan Range, cleanly etched against a bright blue sky.

In an area slightly larger than the state of Arkansas, Nepal boasts the greatest variation in altitude on earth,[1] a terrain so varied and complex it includes a subtropical jungle, the Terai. The Himalayan Mountains, the highest in the world, stretch five-hundred miles across the northern border of the country, Mt. Everest, the tallest, rising to 29,028 feet. The world's deepest valley is also in Nepal, the Kali Gandaki River Gorge, which descends to a depth of nearly four miles.[2]

As rich and as varied as is the scenery of the country, so is its religious life. Two great religions, Hinduism and Buddhism, co-exist peacefully, the gods of each religion often side by side in the country's profusion of temples and shrines. Religious difference is more a topic of conversation in Nepal than any cause for dissent. The country's many ethnic groups commingle peaceably, as well.

Though Nepal is rich in physical beauty and spirituality, it suffers extreme poverty. The World Bank ranks it the fifth poorest nation in the world, its per capita income less than $200 a year.[3] Most of the people work as subsistence farmers, producing barely enough to feed one family. The country's mountainous terrain, along with its few natural resources and high population growth make economic improvement difficult.[4]

Village, Khandbari region.

With the population growing at a rate of 2.6 percent a year, severe demands are placed on the land. Deforestation has become a critical problem with the increased need for fuel, building material, and fodder. As the forests disappear, the waters run off into rivers and streams, carrying valuable top soil with them. The land becomes less fertile, the crops less nutritious, and the people have to spend more time searching for wood and water, walking longer distances, carrying their heavy loads farther. So the quality of life deteriorates. A Gurung hill woman has said it so well, "We need firewood to cook tea, and we need water to cook tea, but when the forests are gone, we won't have either."[5]

Since 1951, when the Shah kings returned to power after a period of corrupt and isolationist rule, there has been a concerted effort to improve the people's lives. The government has instituted five-year development plans, welcoming aid from the developed countries of the world. Efforts are being made in family planning, reforestation, health, education, agriculture, road building, communication, industry, and the development of hydroelectric power. But substantive economic change is slow. Deeply rooted religious and social traditions coupled with the imperatives of subsistence living work against it. Since most Nepalese believe their future is in the hands of the gods (see the tale "Death Invisible," p. 68) and that to alter it would only upset the gods, many are suspicious of change and reluctant to try new ways. Because of the strength of the old ways and the long period of political and economic stagnation brought on by recent rulers, a visit to most areas of Nepal is like traveling back in time. Tourists flock to the country, drawn to its intense spirituality and remarkable landscape, as well as to its many recreational opportunities, such as trekking, white-water rafting, and mountaineering.

Though tourism has become one of Nepal's largest sources of revenue, it has also served to deplete the country's natural resources as Nepal struggles to provide for the influx of visitors. Some Nepalese are ambivalent toward these foreign influences, welcoming their economic input, while at the same time fearing a weakening of the old ways or, worse, their destruction.

It is to be hoped that as the condition of the people improves, their physical environment and culture will remain intact. ❦

The Land and the People

Landlocked Nepal, wedged between China on the north and India on the south, is in the shape of an elongated rectangle, its terrains stretching in distinct east-west bands across the country. In the south lies the subtropical region called the Terai. North of the Terai is an area called the Middle Hills, a mountainous region ranging from five to twelve thousand feet. Above the Middle Hills rise the peaks of the Himalayas, the "abode of snow." Thousands of streams flow from these high mountains into hundreds of rivers, often called Nepal's only natural resource.[6] Bestride these rivers lie beautiful, fertile valleys.

In the south of Nepal, bordering India, is the Terai, inhospitable until the 1950s and 1960s, when mosquito-borne malaria was controlled by spraying. The indigenous people, the Tharus, seem to have a natural immunity to malaria. With the draining of the malarial swamps, the population expanded and diversified as people migrated from India and from the hills above the Terai. Now the Terai is the fastest growing region in Nepal, its fertile land producing a food surplus, primarily rice and sugar cane, which is both exported and transported to other areas of the country. Seventy-five percent of Nepal's industry is in the eastern Terai, where the flat terrain makes it easier to build roads and the proximity to India aids commerce.

Animals of the Terai include the one-horned rhino, elephants, crocodile, deer, water buffalo, sloth bear, and the fast-disappearing tiger, all now protected in Chitwan National Park. The thirty tigers now living in Chitwan make up one-tenth of those left in the world.[7] Once a place of sport for colonial British hunters from India, the Terai now tries to preserve its wildlife species. There are several other wildlife reserves in Nepal and a number of national parks.

North of the Terai, in the Middle Hills, or the Mahabharat Range, the people cultivate the steep slopes by building terraces, thereby extending the arable land. These terraces have been built over hundreds of years and make irrigation easier during the monsoon season. Among the several ethnic groups that live in the Middle Hills are the Magars and the Gurungs, the Rais and the Limbus, whose young men, noted for their soldiering, make up the Gurkha regiments who have aided the armies of Great Britain and India for more than a century. Their soldiering adds to family incomes, so crucial in a subsistence farming economy.

The two most populous valleys of Nepal are nestled in the Middle Hills. The Pokhara Valley, at three thousand feet, is in the center of the country, and the Kathmandu Valley, at four thousand five hundred feet, is in the east. Unique to the Pokhara Valley are several huge lakes, the biggest and most beautiful being Phewatal (see "Lake Phewa," p. 40). Striking

Sherpa herding dzo, *a cross between yak and cattle.*

are the valley's views of the Himalayas, especially the Annapur-na Range and Machhapuchhre, the "fishtail mountain."[8] As a result, Pokhara is the most popular trekking area.

East of Pokhara, in the Kathmandu Valley, three cities form a large population area—Kathmandu, the nation's capital, Patan, three miles south of Kathmandu across the Bagmati River, and Bhadgaon, six miles east of the capital. The myriad temples and shrines of these cities were constructed largely during the fifteenth to seventeenth centuries, a time of great artistic activity when the kings of the Malla dynasty encouraged and supported the Newar craftspeople of the area, who were renowned wood-carvers. The intricately carved windows and doors of Newar buildings remain remarkable in their sense of harmony.

Of the three cities of the valley, Bhadgaon has the fewest new buildings, so it is here that one can truly revel in the old. Happily, foreign aid projects have worked to restore Bhadgaon's medieval streets and architectural treasures. UNESCO (United Nations Educational, Social, and Cultural Organization) has designated seven places in the Kathmandu Valley as world heritage landmarks, a large number considering there are only two hundred such sites in the world. No one country has as many important landmarks in so small an area as Nepal.[9] Still, there is much of the old and the beautiful that is deteriorating.

The Kathmandu Valley is also home to the Tibetan refugee camp Jawalakhel, where Tibetans who fled the Chinese during the 1950s reside. Jawalakhel is an active, thriving community, due in large part to its carpet industry, begun in the 1960s with the help of Swiss foreign aid workers. Here rugs with their traditional colors and designs are kept alive and new ones created.

Beyond Jawalakhel, north of the valleys, rise the Himalayas, covering one-third of the land area of Nepal. On the lower slopes of the foothills the Rai and Limbu people live, expert stonecrafters who build not only the elaborate terraces for farming, but also *chautaras* (see "From the Mango Tree," p. 63), stone walls encircling shady banyan and pipal trees as memorials to the dead. The chautaras are frequently used as rest stops for porters who travel the hillsides bearing heavy loads in woven bamboo baskets strapped across their foreheads. Given the mountainous terrain and sparse road system, porters are an important part of the work force.[10] Some have been carrying heavy loads so long that their foreheads are permanently indented.[11]

In the spring, the lower Himalayas blaze with color as red rhododendron, Nepal's national flower (see "The Uttis Tree," p. 72), blooms. The exuberant display continues through early summer, as different rhododendron species flower.

The Sherpa people, migrants from Tibet over 500 years ago, live between nine to sixteen thousand feet. Most Sherpas retain their Buddhist customs and beliefs. The monastery at Tengboche is testimony to the vitality of their community.

The Sherpa farm during the monsoon season, growing potatoes, buckwheat, and barley in marginal land. At other times of the year, they serve as porters and guides on mountaineering and trekking expeditions. They also herd animals, primarily yak, strong, shaggy, ox-like creatures used for carrying heavy loads and for the milk, meat, and wool they provide.

Other animals of the Himalayas include the snow leopard, the black bear, the flying squirrel, and the legendary yeti, or Abominable Snowman, much talked about, but rarely, if ever, seen. The yeti's large, apelike snowprints have mystified many, but skeptics have explained them as being those of a man merely enlarged in the melting snow.[12]

The peaks of the Himalayas, snow-covered year-round, are believed to be home to the gods. Mt. Everest, or *Sagarmatha*, Roof of the World, stretches more than five miles high. Rivers running southward rib the mountains with gigantic gorges.[13]

Drawn to the formidable challenge of the Himalayas, the mountaineers who scale Mt. Everest receive worldwide attention. The first to climb successfully were the Sherpa Tenzing Norgay and the New Zealander Edmund Hillary in 1953. Other groups followed in quick succession: the Swiss in 1956, the Chinese in 1960, the Americans in 1963, the Indians in 1965, and in 1970 the Japanese, one of whom skied down. The Italians climbed in 1973, and in 1975, the International Women's Year, a group of Japanese women made it to the top.[14]

Records continue to be set, one of the most recent in 1990 marked the ascent of the youngest person ever, a seventeen-year-old French student who climbed with his father, making them also the first successful father and son team. Then, on April 22, 1993, the first Nepalese woman, Pasang Lhumu Sherpa, attained the summit. Unfortunately, she died on her descent because of bad weather.

Mountain climbing and trekking continue to be popular with tourists, and ascents on Everest are scheduled years in advance. A number of peaks, however, are closed to climbing and preserved as holy places.[15]

One final note about the land and its inhabitants—because of the variety of its terrain, tiny Nepal is home to ten percent of the world's bird species.[16] A detailed, colored field guide, *Birds of Nepal* by Robert Fleming, was produced in 1976. 🦜

Religion

Religion informs and plays an integral part in the daily life of Nepal. At the root of most present-day rituals and beliefs lie ancient animist traditions, born from a physical environment both frightening and awesome, to explain the cruelties of the natural world. Animism imbues everything with a spirit—people, animals, mountains, lightning, rain, the tiniest pebble—and demands these spirits be worshiped in order for one to pass through life, and even death, unharmed.

Though animism still holds sway, when Hinduism developed in Nepal in A.D. 300, the people transferred some of their belief in spirits to an omnipotent, omniscient spirit of

Wooden struts of a temple bedecked with carvings of the gods.

the universe called Brahma and to a vast panoply of Hindu gods. Union with Brahma is the aim of Hinduism, a union that can be achieved, the faithful believe, through a series of reincarnations, either up or down the ladder of life, depending upon one's *karma*, or good deeds and thoughts, which include mindful worship of the gods.

Beyond the trinity of Brahma, the creator, Vishnu, the preserver, and Shiva, the destroyer and regenerator, the Hindu gods are legion, each having many incarnations, as well as aspects for good and evil.

The third in the Hindu trinity, Shiva, when incarnated as Pashupati, Lord of Living Beings, is the god most worshipped in Nepal. Other popular gods are Bhairab, a formidable incarnation of Pashupati, and Ganesh, Shiva's son, the elephant-headed god of wisdom. Since Shiva is the god of regeneration, shrines of the male and female symbols, the *lingum* and the *yoni*, are found everywhere throughout the country.

The temple to Lord Pashupati, Pashupatinath, is the holiest Hindu temple in Nepal and is close to Kathmandu. Though only Hindus are allowed in its inner courtyards, everyone can observe the shrines and statues of the outer areas. Around the temple, holy men, called *sadhus* live (see "Lake Phewa," p. 40), ascetics who meditate and offer advice to those who seek it.

The grand temple Pashupatinath is a place where the faithful come to worship every morning before sunrise. It is here they also come to die, to feel for one last time the holy waters of the Bagmati River. Platforms, called *ghats*, extend from the temple out into the river where cremations take place. Hindus believe cremation helps free the soul from the body for the cycle of reincarnation. The ceremony begins when relatives bearing a white-sheeted body draped between two poles run down the hillsides to the temple, a horn announcing their coming. On the temple ghats, the family tends the funeral pyre until there is nothing left but ash. The ashes are then strewn on the waters of the Bagmati, which flow into India's River Ganges, the most sacred of all rivers.

The people who live in the hills cremate their dead on hilltops. And in the high Himalayas, where the earth is too hard to dig, some people bring their dead to the high places and chop them into pieces for the birds to devour.

Though eighty-seven percent of Nepalese practice Hinduism, Buddhism was once the dominant religion, predating Hinduism in Nepal by about 500 years. The two religions have commingled peacefully, the faithful accepting each other's gods and often sharing religious practices and celebrations. Buddhist teachings are widely known and greatly influence Nepalese Hindus, since Buddha is considered to be one of the nine incarnations of Lord Vishnu. There is little orthodoxy in Nepal, most people following whichever gods appeal to them.[17]

Buddhism originated in Nepal through the life and teachings of Siddhartha Gautama, who was born in the Terai in 563 B.C. As a young man, Siddhartha had difficulty reconciling his life of wealth and ease with the suffering he saw around him. He left his family and high station to lead a life of privation and meditation and for six years he pondered life's meaning. Then, with his disciples, he set out to teach others what he had discovered for himself. Called the Buddha, or Enlightened One, his beliefs eventually spread north to Tibet and to other parts of Asia.

Prayer wheels at Swayambhunath stupa.

Some believe that Buddha was trying to restore a sense of morality to religion, which had gotten all tangled up in ritual.[18] Buddhism, more a philosophy than a religion,[19] has been called the rule of the "middle way," or moderation in all things,[20] and stresses the interrelatedness of all things.[21] Its aim is the achievement of *Nirvana*, a state of inner peace. Siddhartha Gautama taught that it is possible to attain Nirvana by giving up an attachment to people and things in a world where nothing is permanent. Meditation and right living help one along this path.

The largest Buddhist shrine in Nepal is the two-thousand-year-old Swayambunath *stupa* just outside Kathmandu. Originally stupas were burial mounds said to house the relics of the Buddha.[22] One interpretation says they were built as representations of the Buddhist view of the universe. They consist of a square base topped by a hemispheric dome, on top of which is another square structure topped by a tiered tower, representing the ladder to Nirvana. From the sides of the square atop the mound, the eyes of the Buddha peer out in four directions. Prayer wheels set in the walls around the stupa are engraved with the Buddhist mantra *om mane padme um* (the jewel is in the lotus). People spin these prayer wheels as they pass by, sending their prayers to heaven. Close by the stupa are a few small monasteries, or *gompa*, where carmine-robed monks are often seen strolling about.

Signs of religious life are not just limited to a few grand temples, but may be seen everywhere throughout the country. Myriad temples and shrines line bustling city streets and quiet country byways. It is said that in Nepal there are more temples than houses. People even have shrines in their homes, often to the spirits of ancestors who need guidance in the afterworld. Worship, or *puja*, is done on a daily basis with offerings of food, flower petals, colored powder, or coins at neighborhood temples and personal shrines. In return, worshippers receive a *tika*, a blesssing of rice grains mixed with red liquid placed in the middle of the forehead to represent the eye of inner vision or wisdom. Sometimes after puja, people sprinkle flower petals in their hair.

The many religious festivals are marked not by an attitude of subdued reverence, but by one of respect, gaiety, and fear.[23] The biggest festival, the Hindu *Dasain* (see "Tuhuro and the Bread-Bearing Tree," p. 93), lasts fifteen days in September and October. Dasain honors Durga, an incarnation of Shiva's wife Parvati, who conquered the evil demon Mahisasura. Durga is represented with each of her many arms holding a weapon, the demon's body at her feet.

During Dasain, people celebrate by coming together with their families and eating special food, showing off new clothing, and watching pageants. Workers get a bonus of one month's pay. On the ninth day of Dasain, animals are sacrificed, their blood dripped over all vehicles, from bicycles to airplanes, to ensure Durga's protection.[24] It is believed that this sacrifice, far from being cruel, is a boon to the animals, releasing their souls for a human reincarnation in the next life. At the end of Dasain, people feel they will be protected from evil for the entire year.

Religion in Nepal, for both Hindus and Buddhists, is a strong physical and psychological presence, the faithful believing that everything one does in this life affects the quality of life in the next. So they set themselves on a path of good deeds and worship in order to achieve either immersion in a higher state or union with a higher being.

It is interesting to note that in the long history of Nepal, not once has there ever been a religious war. ❧

Kathmandu

The bustling, vibrant capitol city Kathmandu is both a religious and a commercial center, a fascinating blend of old and new. Parts of the city are distinctly medieval—dark, narrow passageways winding between wood and brick buildings that seem to lean toward each other, blotting out the sun. The newer areas of the city sport open, airy boulevards lined with modern shops. Over the past ten years the population has grown enormously, bringing woes of traffic congestion and air pollution.

In old Kathmandu, traffic is dense with people and rickshaws, children darting here and there. Burning incense and cook fires sweeten and thicken the air. The noise and bustle increase as the narrow alleyways open onto the market squares and finally onto Durbar Square, the largest of all the markets, alive with street vendors and carpet sellers and bordered by ancient temples. Small girls, their arms covered with thin, brass bracelets, offer trays of sliced mangoes, while kite vendors sell thin paper kites and thick spools of red string.

Many of the temples in Durbar Square are built in the pagoda style, a design created by Nepalese architects to reflect, some say, the beauty and grandeur of the Himalayan pine.[25] Word of the pagoda design spread, and at the end of the thirteenth century the architect Arniko was invited to the king's court in Tibet. From there, the pagoda style spread to China and to other parts of Asia.

The temples and monuments of the area are hardly kept at a reverential arm's length, rather they are a part of people's daily comings and goings. Laundry is draped over statues, and crops laid out to dry on temple and stupa steps. Barbers ply their trade at temple gates, and children crawl about stone monuments as if on a jungle gym. Finely carved stone statuary are marked with dense streaks of colored powder and bits of food and flower petals, signs of continuous worship.[26]

Tucked between the temples of Durbar Square is the Kumari Devi, one of the most exotic dwellings in all of Kathmandu. Inside lives Kumari, the living goddess, a young girl chosen at the age of five for her courage. Legend has it that when the gods were closer to human beings, Kumari came to earth to share her wisdom with the king. When the king expressed a desire for her, Kumari vanished, never to show herself again, except on rare occasions in the guise of a young Newari girl.[27]

All but three days of the year, the Kumari lives behind the walls of her house, visible only to her caretakers. But during Dasain, she is wheeled about the city in a wooden chariot for all to see. Even the king comes out to greet her and bows his head to her in public. When Kumari reaches puberty, another young girl is chosen from a caste of Newar goldsmiths. She must be the bravest of the young contenders and prove herself fearless in a darkened room filled with severed buffalo heads and strange noises.

Close by the dense market squares and alleyways, the wide streets of modern Kathmandu hum with cars and buses, trucks and bicycles. Many stores sell electronic products imported from Hong Kong, and shop after shop offer a wide selection of *sari* (Nepalese dress) material. Luxury hotels rise above the trees, their casinos bustling, their swimming pools filled. Yet in front of these sleek hotels, cows, venerated by Hindus as fertility symbols, wander the streets. And off the modern byways, dirt paths lead to small vegetable markets, where mothers weigh their meager produce, onions, potatoes, and pears, while keeping a watchful eye on their young.

Vegetable seller spreads her wares on temple steps in Durbar Square, Kathmandu.

Kathmandu is a city of striking contrasts, filled with cacophonous noises and pungent smells, a city that assaults the senses and delights and startles the mind. 🐾

History

According to legend, what is now the Kathmandu Valley was once a vast, snake-filled lake, home to many deities. A beautiful lotus plant, a manifestation of the Buddha, grew on the surface of the lake, emitting a strange blue glow. Legend has it that one day a visiting Manchurian *boddhisatva*, or holy man, wanting a closer look at this unusual lotus, plunged his knife into the lake, thereby cutting a huge valley. The waters of the lake rushed out and the sacred lotus plant changed into Swayambhu hill, where Swayambunath, the largest Buddhist stupa, rests today.[28]

Recorded history shows that almost 2,000 years ago, visitors from India to Nepal strongly influenced the religious life of the area. The Indian emperor Ashoka sent missionaries to Nepal to spread Buddhist beliefs. Then one Dharmatta introduced the Hindu religious and caste systems. By A. D. 300 the two religions were strongly in place, though the country remained a collection of tribal principalities and small kingdoms.

Hundreds of years later, in the 1760s, King Prithivi Nareyan Shah, from the Gorkha region between Pokhara and Kathmandu, set out to conquer the disparate kingdoms of the Kathmandu Valley. By 1769 he had accomplished his goal and continued to expand and unify the country, west to Pakistan, east to Sikkim, and south to India. But the British, too, were an expanding empire and met the encroaching Nepalese in a territorial war, which ended in 1816 with the Treaty of Segauli. Though Nepal was forced to retreat, the British were impressed with the Nepalese soldiers and have employed their Gurkha regiments ever since.

The descendants of Prithivi Nareyan Shah, the Shah kings, continued to rule Nepal until 1846, when Prime Minister Jung Bahadur seized power, adding "rana" or "royal" to his name.[29] Rana rule hobbled Nepal and kept it in isolation from the rest of the world for over 100 years. But after World War II, returning Gurkha regiments bringing stories of a better life contributed to a growing discontent. By the late 1940s, the Nepali Congress Party, a moderate socialist group, and a number of leftist parties formed in response to Rana rule, agitating for their removal. In 1951, the Shah King Tribhuvan was reinstated on the throne.

King Tribhuvan died in 1955, but his son Mahendra took over and, in a progressive move, instituted the Land Reform Act of 1957, aimed at weakening the feudal role of rich landlords and limiting rental payments to fifty percent of produce.[30] In 1958, the king called for democratic elections to the parliament, but after only eighteen months he dissolved this body and set up a *panchayat* system of government, allowing for local representation but keeping power in the hands of the king. He promoted this system as being closer to Nepalese political traditions. Political parties were banned and political activists imprisoned.

In 1972, King Birendra succeeded his father and continued the economic development programs. But in 1979, frustrated by their increasing poverty, the citizens demonstrated against their living conditions, and again in 1987, against the autocratic panchayat system of government. The democracy movement grew stronger and more heated, until in 1990 a huge mob headed toward the Royal Palace in protest. The police met the demonstrators with force. Three hundred people were killed, and more than 25,000 arrested. The king was compelled to lift the ban on political parties and a year later, in May 1991, signed a constitution outlining a multiparty democracy, which included civilian control of the military, freedom of expression, an independent judiciary, and universal franchise at eighteen.[31] The democracy movement succeeded in its goal of removing the king's political power without harming him as a symbol of national unity.[32]

A short time after the new constitution was signed, the first fully democratic elections in thirty years were held. The Nepal Congress Party came to power. Three years later, however, the people, frustrated by their continuing poverty and the reported corruption of the administration, voted for the United Marxist-Leninist party, which promised to institute land ownership reform. (Communists in Nepal have been described by political analysts as a moderate group bearing more resemblance to European-style social democrats than to hard-liners.)[33] But nine months later, in September 1995, the UML was toppled by a coalition which included the Nepal Congress Party.

The fledgling democracy is struggling with hard economic realities and, at the same time, trying to forge a path between its two giant neighbors, India and China, in an effort to maintain a position of neutrality and political independence. King Prithivi Nareyan Shah, who united Nepal in the eighteenth century, described the country as a "root between two stones."[34]

One final note. The Nepalese flag, unique with its two attached pennants, bears the sign of the sun and the moon, Buddhist symbols suggesting the hope that Nepal will live as long as these two great heavenly bodies.[35] ❦

Daily Life

The great majority of Nepalese live in rural areas as farmers and herders. The people rise before dawn to gather wood, fodder, and water for their daily needs, often walking great distances carrying heavy loads. These chores done, the morning meal is prepared, typically a grain, some vegetables, such as potato, spinach, or squash, and a legume, most often lentils. The classic Nepalese meal, *dal baat tarkaari*, is lentils over rice with curried vegetables.

Rice is expensive for the ordinary citizen. Cultivated at up to six thousand feet, the large amounts of water borne on the backs of laborers raises the price of the grain. So most people depend on other grains. In the low and middle altitudes, they eat wheat, corn, and millet, and at higher elevations, buckwheat and barley. Grain is ground either by hand or by a water-powered mill, then boiled into a thick paste or cooked into a pancakelike bread called *roti*.

The people of the villages spend their days working in the fields, their children often at their side or tending to the younger ones. Farm work is done by hand, with a simple hoe and a *hansia*, or sickle. Animal-drawn plows are used to till the soil. Most people own only a small plot of land, so they often hire themselves out as farm laborers or tenant farmers. Some even go to work in the cities or to India and send home their earnings. Among the hill people, some are army pensioners who have a money income and often return home and become schoolteachers,[36] passing on to the young what they have learned of reading and writing.

The chores of country life are endless. Besides plowing and planting, people have to churn butter, split firewood, thatch roofs, weave baskets, and tend to their animals. At sunset, the family gathers around the hearth for the evening meal, which is the same as the morning meal. After dinner and some conversation, they sleep.

The many religious festivals and celebrations provide a welcome break from the endless round of chores. Some people enjoy an even longer interruption when they leave their villages to make pilgrimages to holy places. Though life in the country is hard and the material rewards few, many people enjoy a "lightweight heart," as one hill woman has said, because of their simple lifestyle.[37]

Family life in Nepal is the bedrock of community. The generations live together under one roof, grandparents, aunts, uncles, and cousins, the children referring to their relatives using kinship names. For example, a child may call his aunt "father's oldest sister." Attitudes toward elders is respectful, but not all is harmonious in this patrilineal system. Sons sometimes separate from their parents and brothers from each other[38] (see "Two Brothers," p. 57), with the resulting land disputes intense in a country where land ownership is the measure of wealth and social status, for the most practical of reasons.[39]

Young people become directly involved in communal life when they begin working in the fields at around the age of ten or twelve, competing with each other to prove who is the most able and organizing parties to make the work go faster. Courtships often begin in a ritualistic way with the boy chanting a question to a girl. The girl is then required to ply her wit and sing back an answer. If her wit fails, she must agree to marriage.[40]

Children of Bandipur.

On the day of a wedding, the groom, dressed in white, bows his head to his in-laws' feet, then a Brahmin priest sanctifies the marriage. Afterward, the wedding procession begins its journey back to the home of the groom, on the way stopping to sacrifice a goat, given as a dowry (see "Tuhuri and the She-Goat," p. 81) to be eaten at the wedding feast.[41]

Because country life is so intimately tied to the elements, villagers' religious practices in the more remote areas are almost exclusively involved in placating the spirits of the natural world. For example, in areas where hail is extremely destructive, complicated rituals have grown up to ward off its spirit. In all-night ceremonies, villagers gather at the crossroads, where they believe spirits travel, and watch a shaman go into a trance trying to communicate with the spirit of hail.[42]

Since water is a necessity, the people engage in certain rituals to encourage its flow. Some hill people hang bronze bells from stone altars above springs, then dress the surrounding shrubs with sacred thread to placate the *Nagas* (see "The Wish-Fulfiller Shell," p. 33), serpent spirits which control the quality and quantity of water.[43]

Women perform most of the labor in Nepal, in fact, seventy percent of all tasks.[44] Though the constitution declares equality for all people, there remains considerable inequality between the sexes. For example, it falls to Newar women to plant rice. They make the task something of a celebration by dressing up in finery and plaiting their hair with flowers.[45]

Some Brahmin hill women maintain the floors and firepits of their home on a daily basis, rising before dawn to plaster red clay and cow dung on the earthen floors to attract Lakshmi, the Goddess of Wealth. Before eating, they wash their husband's feet and afterward drink the same water.[46]

The birth of daughters goes unheralded. Girl children are seen as burdens and are sometimes fed less[47] and allowed fewer opportunities. In the Terai, dowries must be paid for their marriages, and they always go off to live with their husband's family, where they have to prove themselves through hard work.

In most Indo-Nepalese families, women have little power and divorce is rare. But among some Sherpa groups in the mountains, women are quite powerful, for the men are often away, working as porters or guides on trekking or mountaineering expeditions. Polyandry, usually with the husband's brothers, is not uncommon among these groups. Just so, polygamy among the Indo-Nepalese exists, though illegal, often occurring if the first wife cannot bear a son.

Social stratification extends beyond gender. Among certain Hindu groups, the caste system is observed, a system conferring four levels of status based on the part of Brahma the Creator's body from which ancestors are thought to have sprung. From Brahma's head came the Brahmins, members of the highest caste (see "The River Kamala," p. 61), traditionally the priests. The Chhetris came from Brahma's arms and were the warriors. Today the Brahmins and Chhetris are primarily landowning farmers and tenant farmers, a highly respected profession in Nepal, and they tend to dominate the political scene.[48] From Brahma's belly came the Vaisyas, the tradesmen and artisans, and from his feet, the Sudras, at the bottom of the social ladder yet performing tasks vital to society.[49] These are the goldsmiths, the blacksmiths, the butchers, and the shoemakers.

Adherence to the caste system derives from the Hindu belief in *dharma*, which states that one should play one's proper role in society.[50] The king holds the highest position in this system, since many Hindus believe he is the reincarnation of Vishnu, the protector. Though the caste system in Nepal is not as strict as it is in India, some of the people still hold to certain customs, particularly regarding marriage and eating. Marriage into a lower caste is to be avoided, as is eating with someone of a lower caste. Some believe that boiled rice should be shared only with one's immediate family.[51] But attitudes toward the caste system are changing, and the government has declared the system illegal.

Hill woman selling ginger and turmeric in the Terai.

Nepalese dress varies among ethnic groups. Many Nepalese wear Western garb, but the official government outfit for men is a white Newar suit, a *daura-suruwal*, the pants tight around the lower leg and wide at the top, the shirt loose and colorless, and a Western suit jacket. Traditional dress for women is the *sari*, red being the favorite color, a symbol of joy and happiness in Nepal,[52] though traditional Newar women wear black saris lined with red. Among some women, large amounts of jewelry are popular, their earrings and necklaces handed down from mother to daughter to granddaughter. The official hat of Nepal is a cap called a *topi* (see "The Farmer and the Jackal," p. 53).

Men of Tibetan origin wear a long-sleeved woolen coat called a *chuba*, wrapped so that one shoulder and arm are exposed. Tibetan women wear a blouse, a long woolen jumper, and a multicolored striped apron. Porters typically wear one piece of cloth wound many times around their waist, into which they place their personal belongings, their money, food, pipes, tobacco, and knives.[53]

Newar boy wearing a topi, *the traditional Nepalese hat.*

Housing in Nepal reflects the variety of the terrain. In the Terai, houses are built on stilts as protection against wild animals and the monsoon floods. The people in the mountains also live above ground, on the second floor, their animals on the first, to avoid the cold. For insulation, mountain homes have adjoining walls and roofs made of flat wooden boards that catch the snow. Most houses in Nepal are made of stone or brick and have thatched roofs. Those who are wealthy live in large compounds behind stone walls.

Peculiar to the Newar people of the Kathmandu Valley, and unique in all of Asia, are the three- and four-story red brick houses inlaid with beautifully carved wooden windows and doors. Family compounds are built around a courtyard containing a *chaitya*, or family shrine. The ground floor sometimes has an opening onto the street and may be used as a shop or to store farm equipment or house animals. The floor above is the bedroom, where straw mats are laid out on an earthen floor for sleep. Above that may be a room for visitors, also with straw mats for seating. The top floor is always the kitchen and the family worship center. Sometimes balconies and terraces lined with clay flower pots provide an altogether pleasant aspect. Overhanging roofs protect the floors below and the crowded sidewalks during the downpours of the monsoon.[54]

Inside the home, the hearth is the central gathering place. Here the family comes together and the meals are cooked and served. There are no chimneys in the houses, so as the smoke rises from the hearth, the ceiling is coated with creosote, good protection against bugs and rotting. In most houses, smoke escapes through the windows, but Newar houses have a small hole in the roof covered with a rounded tile, put in place when it rains.

Today only ten out of every hundred people in Nepal live in cities, but there is an increasing urban movement. Like their brothers in the country, city folk rise early, some of the women working over a single burner kerosene stove for two hours preparing the morning meal, which is similar to that eaten in the country—rice with hot curry sauce and a few vegetables. On cold mornings, a cup of hot, steaming tea brewed with milk, sugar, and spices is particularly welcome.

After breakfast, the children go off to school, the more privileged to private English-language schools, the men to their offices. Some women remain at home, making daily trips to the market, since they have no refrigeration and few canned goods. They wash their dishes and do their laundry at a communal tap. By 5 p.m. the men wend their way home. The evening meal is at 8 p.m., and after that everyone goes to sleep. An increasingly wealthy and educated middle class in the cities and towns enjoy lifestyles and aspirations similar to those in the West. These families own stoves and refrigerators, cars and televisions, and encourage their children to get an education and to attend college.

The pace of life in Nepal is slower than in the United States. There are fewer opportunities for recreation, fewer parks and playing fields, fewer commercial centers. Kite flying is popular, as well as other games that do not require expensive equipment, such as *baagh-chaal*, a game like Chinese checkers. Men and boys enjoy playing soccer, volleyball, badminton, table tennis, and follow World Cup soccer with a passion.[55] Though eighty percent of the population goes to school, only a quarter finish fifth grade, so many people cannot read.

Mostly, people spend their leisure time strolling, resting, or talking with friends over a cup of *chiya* (tea) or *chhang* (beer), enjoying the chance to exchange gossip and observe the passing scene. Movies are a popular form of entertainment, primarily the sentimental musicals and action pictures brought up from India. Hindi is close enough to Nepali to be understood. Ticket prices are low and attendance high. Television has become the most popular form of entertainment, however, and seems to be having the most impact on the culture, a satellite bringing Western programs and advertising twenty-four hours a day to a population that, until 1951, did not even tolerate foreign visitors. Nepal Television is increasing its broadcast hours, as well.

Despite the lure of movies and television, the many local and religious festivals continue to have broad appeal and provide a great creative outlet. During these holiday times, most work comes to a standstill, since the people do not wish to offend the gods.[56] The birthdays of Lord Buddha and Lord Krishna are celebrated, along with other gods, as is the king's. There is a mother's day and a father's day and special days for worship of one's brothers, teachers, and ancestors. Many festivals are linked to the agricultural season, such as Machhendranath, a festival to the god of rain and fertility that occurs for one month in the spring.

Life cycle events are celebrated with gusto. In some groups, a baby's naming and destiny, like all important events, are determined by an astrologer according to the position of the planets at the time of birth (see "The Princess of the Vermilion Path," p. 44). The baby's six-month birthday is celebrated with a rice-feeding ceremony. Boys in the Brahmin and Chhetri castes mark their puberty by receiving a gift of a *janai*, a holy thread.[57] The boys are then allowed to eat with the men. In the Hindu and Buddhist tradition, boys at puberty have their heads shaved and go out to beg like the Buddha or a Hindu *sadhu*, or wise man.

For girls, some life cycle events are not as celebratory. The onset of menstruation, among some ethnic groups, brands them as unclean, and they are locked in a room for fourteen days. Before puberty, Newar girls actually have their first marriage[58], wedded to a *bel* fruit, or wood apple, symbolic of a marriage to the soul of their future husband.[59] This allows them greater freedom in subsequent marriages, since the first marriage is considered the most important. In subsequent marriages, therefore, women can divorce, or, if widowed, remarry.

Marriages in Nepal are often arranged, but today more and more people are choosing for themselves. Among some groups, it is the custom to kidnap one's prospective bride for three days. If, at the end of three days, the woman refuses to marry, then that is the end of it.

Typically, women try to have two or more sons and will bear more children with that goal in mind. The fertility rate is 5.7 children per woman. Nepal's high infant mortality rate also encourages frequent pregnancies. Currently because of poor sanitation, one in three children die before age one, and three out of twenty before the age of five.[60] Only twenty-eight percent of the people have access to safe water, the lack of which causes debilitating and deadly diarrheal diseases. Hospitals and clinics are often at a great distance and there are not enough medical practitioners. Traditional healers, called *jhankri* (see "Two Brothers," p. 57), still play an important role in exorcising the evil spirits that cause ill health, which, unfortunately, is rife. Besides diarrheal diseases, people are plagued with elephantiasis, tuberculosis, diseases of the eye, and numerous skin infections.[61] The average life span is fifty-five, low because so many die before the age of five.

Children who are lucky enough to reach the age of five are sent to school, if their labor can be spared. Education is free but not compulsory for eight years, and it is indeed meager. The facilities are few and there is a shortage of teachers and supplies. Classes are often taught outdoors because of crowded classrooms. The literacy rate is low, thirty-eight percent for males and thirteen percent for females. More boys are sent to school than girls. The girls are sent to work.

Despite the fact that many Nepalese live at a subsistence level and have serious health problems and little money, they do not consider themselves poor or deprived.[62] They are a self-reliant people, enjoying the support of their family and community. They remain genial and gentle, their quiet ways and warm smiles only adding to the country's enormous appeal.🐚

Hill woman of eastern Nepal.

The Arts

Art in Nepal is primarily of a religious nature and is found readily in and around the temples. Statues of the gods abound, as do religious paintings called *thankas* which depict the life of Buddha. These are far more common in Nepal than books or newspapers.[63] Temple decoration, most especially the carved woodwork of the doors and windows, and the struts and eaves, are thick with representations of the gods, often depicted with many heads and arms, symbolic of their omniscience and omnipotence.

The gods not only inspire art, it is believed they dispense it as well. To Hindus, music and dance are gifts from the gods to be indulged in at any festive occasion. At religious celebrations, dancers wearing costumes and masks enact the struggles and triumphs of the gods over evil demons.[64] Wandering minstrels, or *gaine*, more common before the advent of radio and television, play their violin-like instrument, the mournfully twanging *sarangi*. Singing competitions are held in certain parts of the country, pitting boys against girls.

Poetry competitions are held, as well. The interest in poetry is so high that Nepal has been called a nation of poets.[65] Competitions are broadcast nationwide on radio and television, and the birthdays of famous poets celebrated with readings and parades. Even the queen writes poetry, some of which has been made into songs.

Like the visual arts, much of the literature of Nepal is religious and comes from the ancient Hindu books, the *Ramayana* and the *Mahabharata*. Since the early twentieth century, however, a modern literature has developed, with poetry its most vital form. In 1979-1980 the Street Poetry Revolution brought two hundred poets to the streets of Kathmandu, reciting poems demanding the abolition of the panchayat system and calling for a more representative government. This movement spread to some fifty towns in Nepal as the Kathmandu poets traveled beyond the valley, encouraging their peers.[66]

The modern short story appeared in Nepal in the 1930s, the product of an educated, urban middle class.[67] In the Western tradition of social, political, and psychological realism, the stories examine aspects of contemporary society, including village life, women, caste, class and ethnic relations, the Gurkha soldier, and tourism. Most literature, however, continues to be dispensed orally through the storytelling tradition. ❦

Storytelling

Storytelling is not only a mode of entertainment, but an important way of passing on a culture's history and values. In Nepal tales are told at religious occasions or whenever a storyteller has the time and inclination, which is mostly at night around the hearth or, during the harvest, in the barn. For children, the favorite time for listening to stories are the few days before and after a full moon. Then, even if it is quite cold, they sit outside around an open fire, a cold breeze at their backs and ears, their hands, feet, face and chest warmed by the fire, the smell of smoke strong in their nostrils. A dog barks in the distance, a woman sings. And the children listen.

Usually it is the elders who tell the tales, but on these cold moonlit nights, the tellers are whoever can endure the frigid air. The listeners indicate their attention by saying "hum," or "yes." This stimulates the teller, who, in turn, tries to make his story even more exciting. Stories are commonly told on the trails as a distraction from the burdens of carrying heavy loads. At these times, tales are called *ukalo bokne namlo*, or "the strap to carry the uphill trail."

We hope you are drawn to these tales and that you gain a glimpse of Nepal, the splendor of its landscape, the spirit of its people. 🍎

Notes

1. Prakash A. Raj, *Kathmandu and the Kingdom of Nepal* (Kathmandu: Naban Publications, 1993), 11.

2. Jeremy Bernstein, *The Wildest Dreams of Kew* (New York: Simon & Schuster, 1970), 8.

3. Raj, *Kathmandu*, 17.

4. Jon Burbank, *Cultures of the World: Nepal* (New York: Marshall Cavendish, 1991), 31.

5. Broughton Coburn, *Nepali Aama, Portrait of a Nepalese Hill Woman* (Santa Barbara, CA: Ross-Erickson, 1982), 74.

6. Burbank, *Nepal*, 14.

7. Bob Gibbons and Bob Ashford, *The Himalayan Kingdoms, Nepal, Bhutan, Sikkim* (New York: Hippocrene, 1983), 98.

8. Raj, *Kathmandu*, 183.

9. Burbank, *Nepal*, 93.

10. Fran P. Hosken, *The Kathmandu Valley Towns* (New York: Weatherhill, 1974), 109.

11. Karl Eskelund, *The Forgotten Valley* (NewYork: Taplinger, 1960), 128, illus. 12.

12. Raj, *Kathmandu*, 203.

13. Bernstein, *Dreams* (New York: Simon & Schuster, 1970), 17.

14. Raj, *Kathmandu*, 199.

15. Lisa Choegyal, *Insight Guides Nepal* (Boston: APA Publications/Houghton Mifflin, 1993), 23.

16. Gibbons, *The Himalayan Kingdoms*, 20.

17. Tony Wheeler and Richard Everist, *Lonely Planet, Nepal* (Hawthorn, Australia: Lonely Planet, 1993), 133.

18. Andrea Matles Savada, ed., Federal Research Division, Library of Congress, *Nepal and Bhutan, Country Studies*, DA Pam 550-35 (Department of Army: 1993), 92.

19. Visual Geography Series, *Nepal in Pictures* (Minneapolis: Lerner Publications, 1989), 44.

20. Wheeler, *Lonely Planet*, 55.

21. Choegyal, *Insight*, 102.

22. Madanjeet Singh, *Himalayan Art* (Greenwich, CT: New York Graphic Society with UNESCO, 1968), 18.

23. Murphy, *The Waiting Land* (New York: Overlook Press, 1987), 30.

24. Burbank, *Nepal*, 110.

25. Hosken, *Kathmandu Valley*, 1.

26. Ibid., 2.

27. Eskelund, *Forgotten*, 150.

28. Gibbons, *The Himalayan Kingdoms*, 39.

29. *Nepal in Pictures*, 29.

30. Gibbons, *The Himalayan Kingdoms*, 53.

31. *Facts on File* 21 September 1990, 708.

32. *Facts on File* 24 November 1994, 887.

33. Ibid., 887.

34. Choegyal, *Insight*, 25.

35. *Nepal in Pictures*, 31.

36. Hosken, *Kathmandu Valley*, 53.

37. Coburn, *Nepali Aama*, 144.

38. Savada, *Nepal and Bhutan*, 83.

39. Ibid., xix.

40. Coburn, *Nepali Aama*, 22.

41. Ibid., 26.

42. Ibid., 157.

43. Ibid., 74.

44. Burbank, *Nepal*, 58.

45. Hosken, *Kathmandu Valley*, 162.

46. Coburn, *Nepali Aama*, 47.

47. Savada, *Nepal and Bhutan*, 86.

48. Karl Samson, *Frommer's Comprehensive Travel Guide, Nepal* (New York: Prentice Hall Travel, 1993), 13.

49. Burbank, *Nepal*, 39.

50. Savada, *Nepal and Bhutan*, 90.

51. Hosken, *Kathmandu Valley*, 111.

52. Raj, *Kathmandu*, 30.

53. Hosken, *Kathmandu Valley*, 110.

54. Ibid., 158.

55. Samson, *Frommer's*, 14.

56. Hosken, *Kathmandu Valley*, 219.

57. Burbank, *Nepal*, 52.

58. Ibid., 52.

59. Wheeler, *Lonely Planet*, 133.

60. Burbank, *Nepal*, 60.

61. Hosken, *Kathmandu Valley*, 162.

62. Ibid., 271.

63. Matti A. Pitkanen, *The Children of Nepal* (Minneapolis: Carolrhoda Books, 1990), 20.

64. Burbank, *Nepal*, 87.

65. Ibid., 88.

66. Michael James Hutt, ed., "The Nepali Literature of the Democracy Movement and Its Aftermath," in *Nepal in the Nineties* (New York: Oxford University Press, 1994), 86.

67. Michael James Hutt, ed. and trans., *Himalayan Voices: An Introduction to Modern Nepali Literature* (Berkeley, CA: University of California Press, 1991), xii. ❦

Mt. Everest, the world's tallest mountain, rises to 29,028 feet.

Hills terraced for farming in the Kathmandu Valley.

Rooftop view of Kathmandu and the surrounding valley.

Buddhist monastery Tengboche (12,716 feet) after a light snowfall.

House on terraced slope, Khandbari region. Bottom floor shelters the animals.

Newar farmer in the city. A *tika*, the sign of worship, is on his forehead.

Gurung village north of Pokhara in the Annapurna Range.

Teej, the Festival of Women, when women and girls gather at Pashupatinath Temple wearing the red and gold *saris* in which they were wed in order to honor married life.

Village girl of the Kathmandu Valley in traditional dress.

Sherpa children in the Himalayan village
Namche Bazaar, 11,000 feet.

The rhododendron, Nepal's national flower, blooms on the lower slopes of the Himalayas.

Pagoda-roofed temples in downtown Kathmandu.

The all-seeing eyes of the Buddha peer out at Swayambhunath stupa, as prayer flags flutter in the breeze.

Statue of Bhairab, the fearsome incarnation of Shiva. Patan.

Bas reliefs of the Buddha sculpted in a temple wall.

Entrance to Hindu temple, Durbar Square, Patan.

The Tales

The Wish-Fulfiller Shell

All day Kaude worked in his father's rice fields on the terraced mountain slope. His back bent under a hot sun, he planted the green shoots in the muddy soil. From time to time he straightened and looked out at the peaks of the snow mountains, brilliant in the distance.

Kaude and his father were happy together, but they were very poor. They had only a few fields of rice, three chickens, and a small, wooden hut. One day Kaude said to his father, "I must leave our village and go out to seek my fortune. I may have luck and bring back riches."

Now Kaude's father had three hundred *rupees*, a small amount he had been able to save. He gave this to the boy, and the two embraced. Then Kaude started on his way.

After several days, Kaude came to a village where he saw a man kicking a cat. "Brother, why do you kick this cat?" Kaude asked.

"She steals my yogurt, spills my milk, and eats everything in sight," the man complained.

"If you let the cat go, I will pay you one hundred rupees for your trouble," Kaude said. Gladly the man took the money and let the cat go. Then Kaude continued on his journey, the cat following close behind. Through forests and villages they walked, and up and down mountains.

After several days Kaude came upon a man who was beating a dog. "Brother, why do you beat this dog?" Kaude asked.

"Because he makes too much noise and he dirties my house," said the man.

"I will pay you one hundred rupees if you let him go." The man was more than happy to get so much money for the troublesome creature.

---

rupee—a small sum of money

Now Kaude continued on his way, the cat and the dog following close behind. For several days they walked, past temples and *stupas*, beneath the all-seeing eyes of the Buddha. Soon they came to a village where they saw a man chasing a mouse. "Brother, why do you chase this mouse?" Kaude asked.

"Because he eats my grain and nibbles my clothing," the man complained.

Kaude paid the man one hundred rupees and the mouse was set free. Now Kaude had no money, but the mouse, the cat, and the dog were his friends. They walked on together until the animals were so tired they could walk no more. They lay down beside a pond beneath a *pipal* tree and quickly fell asleep. Kaude rested beside them.

Suddenly Kaude was startled by a voice from the pond. "I am King of the *Nagas*," the voice said, "serpent god of the Underworld. I have heard of your kindness to the animals. Now take this magic shell and throw it in the air, and whatever you wish shall be granted."

Just then Kaude felt a small shell in his hand. He was feeling hungry, so he threw the shell in the air, saying, "A delicious rice pudding for everyone." Immediately a large bowl of rice pudding appeared. Kaude could not believe his eyes. He awakened the animals, and they ate until they could eat no more.

Then Kaude said, "I must go home to my father and share my good fortune. Thank you for your company, my friends. I hope all be well with you. But if ever you should fall into trouble, come to me, for I will always help you."

---

stupa—a Buddhist shrine

pipal—banyan tree

Naga—serpent linked with obscure forces of the underworld which guards the treasures hidden in the womb of the earth and the springs which give it life

When Kaude arrived home, his father ran out to greet him. The two joyfully embraced. Then Kaude threw the magic shell in the air, saying, "For my father, a magnificent palace." At once an enormous palace rose up before them. The old man could not believe his eyes and thanked his god for the miracle.

The years passed and Kaude grew to be a handsome young man, the richest in the country. Still he showed kindness wherever he went.

One day his father said to him, "I am growing old and would like to see you marry. I have heard the king's daughter is the most beautiful in the land. Shall I ask for her hand on your behalf?"

"You may go to the king," Kaude said, "for I have heard that the princess is loving and joyful." The old man went to the palace and found that, indeed, the king had heard of Kaude's great wealth. He readily agreed to his daughter's marriage, but on one condition.

"Whoever wishes to marry the princess," the king said, "must pave the streets of the capital with gold." The old man knew that with the magic shell his son could do anything.

"Your wish shall be granted," the old man said.

"Then let it be," said the king, "and your son shall marry my daughter." The prime minister, on hearing the king's words, ran from the room. He had always dreamed that one day his own son would marry the princess. He knew he had to act quickly.

When the prime minister found his son, he said, "A man from another village has dazzled the king with his riches. He will marry the princess unless you act now. Go to this Kaude's house disguised as a peddler, and discover the secret of his wealth." The minister's son did as he was told. Disguised, he ran to Kaude's house and hid in a cupboard in the young man's room.

That night when Kaude entered his bedchamber, he pulled the magic shell from under his pillow and threw it in the air, saying, "Pave the road to the palace with gold." Instantly, the road to the palace was covered with gold. Kaude then placed the shell beneath his pillow and went to sleep, dreaming of the lovely princess.

The minister's son waited until he heard Kaude breathing deeply. Then slowly he inched his hand under the pillow until he touched the magic shell. Carefully he removed it and tiptoed from the room.

The minister's son ran from the palace and, when he was at some distance, he threw the shell in the air, saying, "Make Kaude's riches vanish and bring them all to me. Then take me to a mountain top and carry in the princess." The magic shell did as it was told.

The next morning, Kaude and his father awoke to find themselves back in their old hut, the chickens wandering in and out of the doorway. They were as poor as they once had been. Now Kaude decided he had to once more leave his village and go out in search of fortune. He embraced his father and set out across the valley.

For many days, Kaude walked, until one day he came upon his old friends, the cat, the dog, and the mouse. They were delighted to see each other and told each other everything that had happened since they had last been together.

When the animals finished their stories, Kaude told his. After he had finished, he stood up and bade them farewell. The animals watched as slowly he walked down the road, his back bent, his shoulders stooped. "Kaude looks so downcast and weary," said the dog. "We must try to help him." "Yes," said the cat. "We must find the magic shell." The mouse was already hurrying off. He called back over his shoulder, "Come, friends, we haven't a minute to lose."

Quickly the animals traveled through the villages and forests of the foothills. After many days, they came to the mountains. On the top of one, they saw a palace glittering above the snow. They knew this must be Kaude's and that inside lay the magic shell.

They began to climb, higher and higher, above the trees to where the snow began. After days of climbing, they finally reached the top. The palace rose up before them. The dog lost no time in rushing to the gates, but the guard kicked him aside and sent him sliding.

"No dogs allowed!" the guard snarled.

Then, meowing sweetly, the cat padded up to the watchman. He looked down at her and said, "Open the gates. She will be good at killing the rats." Quickly the cat padded into the yard and up the steps of the palace. She searched the hallways and passageways until she found the room of the minister's son. The young man was almost asleep, but before closing his eyes, he took the magic shell from his pocket and put it in his mouth. The cat watched carefully, then ran to tell the others.

"I have a plan," said the mouse, when the cat had finished. "When the minister's son is asleep, I will tickle his nose with my tail. He will sneeze, his mouth will fall open, and the shell will come flying out. You, cat, must then pick up the shell and run off with it."

The next night, the cat and the mouse approached the palace stealthily. The mouse scurried in under the gate, the cat chasing after. The watchman, looking on, laughed loudly. "See, she is at it already!" he bragged. The two animals ran into the palace and down the long corridor to the room of the minister's son. Soon after, the young man entered his room. He had just finished eating a huge meal and was feeling very sleepy.

"Ahhh, how happy I am," the minister's son sighed. "I am the richest in all the kingdom, and I will always be so. If the princess only loved me, my happiness would be complete. But she waits for Kaude. She has heard he is the kindest in the land. Ah, me. Some day she will forget him and marry me." With that, he popped the shell in his mouth and fell asleep.

"Now!" whispered the mouse, as he swished his tail back and forth under the nose of the minister's son. "Haak chi yummm!" The minister's son sneezed loudly. The shell flew out, the cat picked it up, then ran from the room, the mouse following close behind.

The cat and the mouse slipped under the palace gates to where the dog was waiting. Then all three hurried down the mountain until they came to a river. The cat hopped on the dog's back, the dog took the mouse carefully in his jaw and started to swim across.

After a time, the dog, feeling uncomfortable, shifted a little. The sudden movement frightened the cat, who called out, "Take care or I may drown!" As the cat spoke, the shell fell from her mouth. To her dismay, a fish swimming by swallowed it. The disheartened animals reached the other side of the river and sat silently on the bank. After a time the cat spoke.

"It is I who lost the shell, so it is I who must find it." Across the river she spied an otter sunning himself on the bank. "I will ask the otter for his help," she said. She called and the sleek animal swam to her. After listening to her story, he dived in the river and immediately caught the fish who had swallowed the shell. He tossed it up on the bank. Just then a hawk swooped down and, landing on the fish, made off with it. The animals were struck dumb.

After a time the mouse said, "I have a plan. I will lie by the river and pretend to be dead. The hawk will be tempted and will fly down to pluck me up. You, cat, must then pounce on him and hold him tight."

The mouse then lay by the riverbank, and, just as he had predicted, the hawk, circling overhead, spied him and came rushing down. Immediately, the cat pounced on the hawk's back and held him, while the dog cried out, "Give up the fish or the cat will dig her claws in deeper." The hawk, eager to be rid of the sharp-clawed cat, spit out the fish and flew off.

The mouse then turned to the fish, who lay gasping on the bank. "Give up the magic shell or we will leave you to die." The fish quickly gave up the shell, and the dog dropped her back in the river.

Now the animals ran for seven days and seven nights, not stopping for food or rest, until they came to the hut of their beloved Kaude. Kaude had returned home, weary from his travels, and once again was working in his father's rice fields. You can imagine his surprise when the cat, the dog, and the mouse appeared before him and dropped the magic shell at his feet.

He had given up all hope of ever seeing the shell again. Immediately he threw it in the air, shouting, "Rice pudding for everyone!"

The shell did its work. As they ate, Kaude turned to the animals and said, "Dear friends, for all you have done, I will reward you with riches for the rest of your days." Then he threw the shell in the air, saying, "My palace and my stables." On the spot, his wish was granted.

Just then, on a far-off mountain top, the minister's son awoke, his mouth feeling strangely empty. He realized the magic shell had disappeared. Frantically he looked about him, but all he could see were the clouds and the white peaks of the snow mountains. He knew he was alone and with nothing.

Slowly he came down the mountain. When he reached the river, rushing and roaring, he found he was unable to cross. So the minister's son had to live out his days in a strange land.

The princess, who had been asleep in the palace, awoke and looked about her. To her surprise, she saw she was no longer on the mountain top but in a pleasant valley. She stepped from her room into a garden, where she saw a young man walking with three animals. Kaude rushed to her. "I am delighted to see you," he said. "I am Kaude, and I hope some day we will marry."

"I have heard of your kindness," said the princess. "I will marry you with great happiness." So on a fortunate day, Kaude and the princess were married.

They lived contentedly for the rest of their lives, bringing joy and good fortune to their subjects and always helping the needy who came to their door. 🐚

Lake Phewa

Story Note: *In the mountainous areas of Nepal, it is difficult to find shelter for the night. This story emphasizes the importance of keeping one's door open to the traveler.*

Deep in the Pokhara Valley lay a village filled with hardhearted people. One evening a wandering *sadhu* came to this village as darkness was settling on the land. Since he could go no farther, he went up to the house of a villager and asked if he could stay the night. The villager slammed the door in his face, crying, "Go away from my door."

It is the custom in Nepal to always open the door to a visitor. As the ancient saying goes, *"Atithi devo bhava."* ("The guest is like a visiting god.") But the people of the village were hardhearted and did not respect this tradition of hospitality.

The wandering sadhu then went to every house in the village, asking, *"Bas paincha?* ("May I have shelter for the night?") But in every house, the answer was the same. "Go away from my door!"

Now the sadhu realized that, though it was completely dark, he must continue on his journey. He came to the edge of the village and spied a small old hut with crumbling walls. "Why should anyone offer me shelter here, when others in much grander houses have turned me away?" said the sadhu. He went by the house without stopping.

Suddenly he heard a voice calling, "Who is that walking by in the darkness?" The sadhu turned and saw in the dimness an old woman standing in the doorway.

---

sadhu—holy man

bas paincha? Is there shelter for the night?

"Oh, mother," replied the sadhu. "I am a wandering sadhu."

"Why are you not settled in for the night?" asked the old woman.

"Because no one in your village would give me shelter," the sadhu replied, "so I must walk on."

"You cannot do that," said the old woman. "Please, come into my hut and share my food with me."

"Why, thank you, mother," said the sadhu, as he entered the old hut. "How is it that a kind person like yourself lives in such a village of hardhearted people?"

"Oh, great soul," said the woman, "you know that it is the *Kaliyug*, the Time of Evil. So I cannot blame the people." The old woman then set about preparing the little food she had, not even enough for one person. When she had finished, she turned to the sadhu and said, "You may wash your hands, oh, great soul. Your food is ready."

The sadhu washed his hands and sat down to his meal. He soon saw, however, that the old woman was crying. "What is wrong, oh, mother?" asked the sadhu.

"Nothing, great soul. It is just that I wish I could serve you better with more plentiful food."

"Come now," said the sadhu. "I am a wanderer and sometimes go to sleep with no food at all. Why, this is a feast!" The old woman served the sadhu, waiting to eat herself, as was the custom. But when the sadhu had finished, he realized the old woman had saved nothing for herself. "Oh, mother," said the sadhu, "you should not have served me all of your food."

"But great soul," said the woman, "it is my *dharma* to feed my guest." The old woman then gave the sadhu a mat to sleep on. He took it to the porch and went to sleep. During the night, it began to rain. It rained so hard, the old roof leaked. By morning, the old woman and the sadhu were soaked.

Kaliyug—The Iron Age, a time of man's inhumanity to man. In this age, man eats meat and dairy products in great quantity and may even eat human flesh. Some believe that after all the human meat is eaten and there are no people left, the *Satyayuga*, the Age of Truth, will begin (Coburn, p. 41).

dharma—holy deed

Now the sadhu had to be on his way. He thanked the old woman for her kindness, whereupon she clasped his hands, saying, "Please come and visit me whenever you are in this village." The sadhu smiled, but his eyes were sad.

"No one will ever walk this land again," he said. "Today the lake above the village will break through and the entire valley will be flooded. The narrow gorge at the end of the valley will be blocked by earth and boulders, and the village will become a lake. You must leave this valley today, oh, mother." The sadhu then bade farewell to the old woman and went on his way.

Quickly the old woman left her hut and went to tell the villagers what the sadhu had predicted. "You must leave this place at once," said the old woman, "for the waters of the lake will soon spill over into the valley and all will be washed away." No one listened to her.

Instead they mocked her, saying, "Too long she sits in that broken-down hut to know what she is talking about!" They laughed. "What does an old woman know anyway?"

The old woman felt sorry for the people, because she knew she could not help them. Alone, she started to leave the valley, climbing up the steep mountain slopes. Suddenly she heard a roar and turned to see the natural dam of the lake above crumbling, the water from the lake flowing over the sides of the cliff into the valley. "Oh, *Ram*!" cried the old woman. "Please help these poor people!"

The woman looked again and saw that the dam had all but disappeared. The water was now pouring down the cliff into the valley with a great roar. Above the noise of the falling water, the old woman heard the villagers calling to their gods. To her dismay, she saw their huts, their cattle, and their farms all being swept away in the rushing water. In no time, the narrow gorge at the end of the valley was blocked with earth and boulders. Just as the sadhu had said, the water was beginning to rise. The people of the village were trying to escape the valley, but they were caught in the rising waters and drowned.

Ram—Lord Rama, hero of the *Ramayana* and the seventh incarnation of Lord Vishnu

"Oh, Rama, Rama!" the old woman cried out in despair. Suddenly she saw that she too might be caught in the rising flood. She hurriedly scrambled up the cliff, the water lapping at her feet.

Higher and higher she climbed, and when she felt she could climb no more, she saw a rock in the shape of a boar's head and clasped it tightly. Then, as suddenly as the waters had risen, they stopped, and the woman saw that the flood was calm. Thanking her god, she worshipped the boar's head rock, knowing it was Lord Baraha the boar, third incarnation of Lord Vishnu.

To this day, deep in the Pokhara Valley in western Nepal, you can see the stone boar's head rising out of *Lake Phewa*. The people of the area worship this stone and tell the story, as they have for generations, of the rising waters of the lake and the old saying, "The guest is like a visiting god." 🍂

Lake Phewa or *Phewatal*—the biggest and most beautiful of the five lakes in the Pokhara Valley

The Princess of the Vermilion Path

Story Note: *The princess of the vermilion path is symbolic of the beauty of youth and of the embellishments of the storyteller. The most highly regarded storytellers in Nepal are those whose mouths drip with flowers, whose stories, while fulfilling the requirements of the most effective cautionary tales, are told in beautiful language and melodious tones, instructing both morally and aesthetically.*

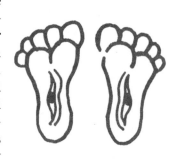

Once there lived a kind and charitable king who welcomed everyone to his palace. One day a *saint* came to the palace door asking for food, and the king served him a delicious meal. The saint was well pleased. "For your generosity," said the saint, "I will bestow a blessing upon you. Soon you will have a daughter with all *thirty-two good qualities*." True to the saint's words, nine months later, the queen gave birth to a beautiful baby girl.

Now the king was eager to learn his daughter's destiny, so he assembled all the learned *jyotshies* of his kingdom. He listened as they told him her future. Indeed, she was born with all thirty-two good qualities, they assured him, and wherever she went, she would bring good fortune.

One of the most learned of the jyotshies added, "When the girl turns sixteen, she will experience some astonishing changes. When she speaks, beautiful flowers will fall from her mouth. When she smiles, her face will become as luminous as the moon. When she cries, pearls will fall from her eyes. And when she walks, she will leave a path of vermilion powder.

---

saint—holy man

thirty-two good qualities—Hindus believe that the perfect person has all thirty-two good qualities, including kindness, patience, courage, and wisdom

jyotshi—fortune teller

The king was well pleased with the jyotshi's predictions but was curious about one thing. "Whom will my daughter marry, oh learned soul?" asked the king.

Quickly the jyotshi made some astronomical calculations and said, "Oh king, she will marry a young prince, wise and brave like herself, who will have all thirty-two good qualities. He will come from the south."

"How will I know him?" asked the king. "If my daughter is so outstanding, won't she have many suitors?"

"Do not worry, my king," said the jyotshi. "Just follow my instructions. When your daughter reaches the age of sixteen, you must hide her from everyone. Her astonishing qualities must be kept secret. The right prince will come to marry her on his own. If you must bring the princess before any one, disguise her face with paint and teach her to communicate only with signs."

"Then how will the real prince find her?" asked the king.

"Trust my words, oh king," said the jyotshi. "In his wisdom, he will find her." Pleased by the jyotshi's words, the king rewarded him with riches.

The years passed and the little princess grew happily. On her sixteenth birthday, the jyotshi's predictions came true. As the princess walked, she left traces of vermilion powder. When she smiled at the pretty red path, she saw the room lit with a gentle moonglow.

"Oh, look what is happening, mother!" the princess cried, and as she spoke, beautiful flowers fell from her mouth. Now the princess was frightened and began to cry. Then another strange thing happened. Instead of tears, pearls fell from her eyes. "Oh, mother, mother!" the princess called.

She ran to her mother, pearls raining from her eyes, flowers springing from her mouth, and leaving a path of vermilion powder. The queen mother was amazed at the splendid sight of her daughter and hugged and kissed her, tears of pleasure in her eyes.

"Do not worry, my darling," said the queen. "What is happening to you was predicted at your birth by the jyotshies. They said that at the age of sixteen you would be thus blessed. These are the signs of your divine qualities, my darling. You are the only one in all the world who has them."

The king now hurried to his daughter's side. "My princess," he said, "the learned jyotshi urged us to keep your amazing qualities secret, so that no ordinary man would come asking for your hand.

You must hide your luminous smile, your tears of pearls, your flower-borne speech, and your footsteps of vermilion powder until the real prince, who is your destiny, finds you."

Now that very day, in the south, a wise and handsome young prince dreamed of a beautiful princess whose smiles were as luminous as the moon, whose speech was embroidered with flowers, whose tears were pearls, and whose footsteps left streaks of vermilion powder. At the end of the prince's dream, a saint appeared telling him he was destined to marry the princess.

"She is in the north," said the saint. "Go and find her." The prince arose from his bed, puzzled by his dream but unable to forget the princess. Days passed, and still he thought of her. One day he decided he must go and seek the beautiful girl in the north.

Soon after, the prince's father, who was able to understand the speech of animals, was visited by a crow. "King," the crow said, "your son has decided to travel to the north. He will suffer in his endeavors. You must give him your sword."

The prince's father then went to his son, saying, "I am proud of your bravery and your willingness to seek your destiny. Take my sword with you. It will be a help to you."

"I have my own sword, father," said the prince, "and I am used to it. Why do you offer me yours?"

"My son," said the king, "mine is no ordinary sword. It is a sword powerful enough to break a mountain. Take it with you." The prince, accepting his father's sword, bade him farewell.

For many days and nights the prince traveled northward. In each kingdom he stopped at the royal palace asking for water. He had one rule—he would accept water only from an unmarried person.

When he came to the princess' kingdom, he went, as usual, to the royal palace and asked for water. The queen met him at the palace door and offered him some. "Oh, queen, I do not accept water from the hands of one who is married," said the prince. "Please send water with an unmarried soul, or I will go away from your door."

Now the king and queen were in a dilemma, for their daughter was the only unmarried soul in the palace. The king went to meet the prince. "My dear stranger," he said, "please take water from me. Unfortunately, we have no unmarried person in the palace."

"I do not drink water from a married person, oh king," the prince repeated. "But do not trouble yourself, for I will find another household and ask them for water. Truly I thank you."

Now the king and the queen were very sad, for no one had ever gone unsatisfied from their door. The king begged the stranger, "Stay a moment. You cannot leave without having water."

The king and queen then decided to let the princess bring the water to the stranger. First they painted her face and told her, "Take this water to the stranger at the door, pretty one. But do not speak a word to him. Come back as soon as he has finished."

The princess nodded and took the water. When she reached the palace door, the prince saw a girl whose face was painted and who was holding a jar of water. She did not speak a word. "Why are you silent?" asked the prince. "I will not accept the water unless you speak to me." The princess signed to the young man that she could not speak.

The prince did not believe her and, looking closely, saw that, although she was painted, she was quite beautiful. He saw at her feet marks of vermilion powder. Then he knew this was the princess of his dream, but he had to be certain.

"I do not drink water from a pot," said the prince to the princess. "Please pour it into my palms so I may drink of it there."

The prince then extended his hands and the princess poured the water into them. When his hands were filled, the prince suddenly splashed the water onto the princess' face. The paint washed away, revealing the princess' beauty.

Now the princess was dismayed. "What have you done to me, stranger?" she said. "Is this how you repay our generosity? No one has ever treated us so." As the princess spoke, flowers floated from her mouth.

The prince was both happy and amazed. "Beautiful princess," he said. "Forgive me my meanness. I met you in a dream and left my country to find you. I have come to marry you."

"Who are you?" asked the princess. "How is it that you propose marriage at first glance?"

"I am a prince from a southern kingdom, my princess. My father is king and my country prosperous. As you can see, you and I will make a good match."

"Do not talk to me of your father's prosperity," said the princess. "I am not interested in fortune. I will marry only a person who can stand on his own. I will marry the bravest man in all the world."

"I will endure anything to marry you," said the prince. The king then came to the door and spoke to his daughter.

"You need not test him, my dear," said the king, "for the great jyotshi predicted the destined prince would recognize you. He is indeed the one."

"Oh, noble king," said the prince, "you need not speak for me. I welcome your daughter's challenge and will prove my bravery."

"Then let it be," said the king.

The next day the princess called for the best smiths of the kingdom to build seven iron chambers. She called the country's magicians to fill each chamber with ghosts and evil spirits. In the last chamber, she placed a *mohar*, a gold coin stamped with the royal sign. Then she proclaimed to all the people, "He who brings me this mohar, I will marry."

News traveled quickly throughout the kingdom and soon reached the other kingdoms in the north and south. In no time, all the kings and princes of the world had heard about the wonderful princess and all wanted to marry her. Many of them rushed to her kingdom and into the mysterious chambers, but not one came out. After many days, the king said to the prince, "Why are *you* not trying to win the mohar as the others have done? Are you afraid?"

"No," said the prince. "I will risk my life for your daughter's hand, but I am allowing the others to satisfy their desires first."

"You are indeed noble," said the king, "but already a thousand suitors have entered the chamber and not one has come out. There are no more candidates, so it is your turn to go into the chambers and fetch the mohar. Then I will arrange the wedding feast."

"I will go now," said the prince. The prince then walked into the first chamber. Quickly the door closed behind him. It was dark inside, and though the prince could not see anything, he heard voices calling, "We were so foolish to fall into the princess' trap."

"She is nothing but a witch."

"Why did I fall in love with such a cruel one as she?"

Their helpless cries touched the prince, but he was neither sad nor afraid. Instead, he removed his father's sword from its sheath and struck it to the ground. Fire suddenly flared up, and the prince saw in its light hundreds of men crawling along the floor, struggling to find their way out. Hundreds more lay unconscious.

One of the suitors spoke up, "Oh, great one, who are you? Your fire has made me hopeful we are not lost." The brave prince then struck the ground again and the fire flared higher. Now he saw a torch attached to the wall and lit it. The suitors gathered around him.

The brave prince spoke, "Dear friends, do not accuse the princess, for she is only trying to find her equal. I will rescue you, but first I must pass through the seven chambers and bring back the mohar."

"Don't be silly," said a suitor. "If you know a way out, help us to escape. Do not go further into the chambers."

"I am sorry," said the brave prince, "but I must." The prince then went to the second door and read what was inscribed: "Proceed courageously, and you will be rewarded. Step back like a coward, and you will be killed." The brave prince struck the door with his sword. It opened with a sound like thunder. Hundreds of ghosts flew out, small ones, large ones, some with eyes and mouths in their bellies, some mere skeletons.

The suitors were fearful, but the prince covered them with his sword and drew a circle around them. The mark of the circle began to burn and the ghosts and the spirits sprang back. "You are safe now," said the prince to the suitors. "In a few days I will return with the mohar."

He then stepped out of the circle, and the ghosts attacked him. He hit them with his sword and, strange to see, every one of them turned into a piece of ragged clothing.

The prince entered the second room and broke down the third door, whereupon thousands of fire-ghosts rushed out at him. The whole room was burning and the prince could not find his way. The ghosts tried to burn him too, but the prince jumped into their midst and began slashing at them with his sword. Suddenly the fires dwindled and the fire-ghosts turned to ash.

The prince then stepped forward and broke down the fourth door. Suddenly he was hit with a wall of water that almost drowned him. He flailed at the wall with his sword, and in an instant the flood waters became vapor.

Again the prince stepped forward and broke down the fifth door. This time, boulders tumbled out upon him, and he was almost buried. But he fought back with his sword and the boulders turned to sand.

Again the prince stepped forward and broke down the sixth door. Now lions and tigers swarmed upon him, elephants and bears, snakes and scorpions, vultures, mosquitoes, and wasps. The prince was in pain and was suffering, but still he was not afraid. He pierced every creature with his sword and fought for seven days and seven nights until all the animals were but a stack of dry hay.

When he felled the last animal, the seventh door opened, and the prince saw inside the mohar, as brilliant as a burning fire. He stepped forward to seize it but suddenly he was surrounded by beautiful maidens, offering him fresh fruit and cool water. The prince tried to brush past them and reach for the coin, but the maidens stood like a gate before him. "Why do you hurry, brave prince?" they asked. "Please stay and enjoy this food. It is all for you."

"Dear ladies, I have a purpose," said the prince, "and I will not be detained."

"Prince, here in our world no one dies. Everyone lives forever. Stay with us and rule over us."

"Thank you for your offer, kind ladies," said the prince, "but I cannot stay. I am a human from an earthly world and am therefore destined to die. I cannot leave my people, my family and friends. Most of all, I cannot leave the princess whom I plan to marry. I must go back."

The maidens closed in a tighter circle around him. "Why is it you want only one lady?" they asked. "Look at us. We are as beautiful as the princess. You could marry us all."

"Please do not force me to hurt you, beautiful ladies," said the prince. "Though you propose to kill my will, I must move forward and retrieve the coin." The maidens blocked his way, their arms outstretched, pleading, "Please, do not leave us. Stay with us. Stay."

The prince pushed the maidens aside with his sword and suddenly they turned into silken swaths of cloth.

Now the prince did not waste a moment. He plucked up the golden mohar, and in an instant everything he had touched with his sword vanished—the silken cloths, the grains of sand, the ashes, the vapors, the ragged clothing. The prince hurried back to the first room where the suitors were waiting.

"Friends," he said, "follow me. I will break down the door and you all will be set free." With that, the prince struck the door with his sword and it fell apart with a clap of thunder. On the other side stood the king and queen. The suitors, frantic to escape the iron chamber, pushed past the prince, causing him to drop the mohar. Then they all rushed to get it, scrambling in the dirt, each one claiming the coin was his. The brave prince remained apart, saying not a word.

Disgusted by the spectacle, the king went up to the prince and said, "It was you who broke through the chambers and brought back the coin. Why then don't you claim it?"

"My king," said the prince, "the princess has tested my bravery. Now I will test her wisdom. Let us see how she discovers who is the bravest among us." The princess smiled, her face lit with a silvery glow. She spoke in a shower of beautiful flowers.

"Tomorrow morning, everyone who is my suitor will come to the courtyard. I will then discover which of you is the brave soul who has brought back the mohar."

The next day the princess sat in the courtyard, surrounded by ragged clothing, ashes, sand, vapors, hay, and silken cloths. "He who recognizes these things," said the princess, "is the bravest and the one I will marry."

The king added, "And the person who fails to recognize these things will be hanged." The suitors mumbled among themselves, laughing at how simple it would be to identify the few items. They then quarreled as to who would go first.

One by one, they came before the princess and, pointing at each item, said, "This is ragged clothing, these are ashes, this vapor, this sand, this hay, and these are bits of fine cloth."

Finally, at the end of the long line, the prince came before the princess. Pointing at each item, he quickly said, "These are ghosts. These are fire-ghosts. This is water. These are boulders. These are animals. These are maidens."

The princess clapped her hands and announced joyfully, "Indeed, you are the bravest of all, my prince. It is you whom I will marry." As she spoke, flowers floated from her mouth.

"Bravo!" cried the king. "There will be a marriage ceremony the likes of which no one has ever seen." Then he turned to the suitors and snarled, "But first we must hang the cheats!" The suitors fell at the king's feet.

"Have mercy, oh king," they pleaded. "Forgive us. Please spare our lives so that we may honor you for the rest of our days."

The brave prince spoke, "Just king, please forgive them on this joyous occasion."

The king, touched by the brave prince, said, "You are the one who has rescued them, yet they tried to cheat you. Still you want to forgive them? Noble prince, you are not only the bravest, you are the kindest. I am grateful my daughter will marry you. May you live a long and fruitful life together." The king then forgave the suitors, who vowed to pay tribute to the brave prince as their emperor.

The king arranged for the wedding banquet, the likes of which has never been seen, then and now. 🦋

The Farmer and the Jackal

Once in a certain village there lived a poor farmer who had only a hen and a field of corn. One day the hen began laying eggs, and the farmer was overjoyed. He took a few of the eggs for his supper and left the rest for the hen to hatch. Baby chicks soon pecked out, as the farmer looked on happily.

Someone else was also watching from the nearby woods, his eyes wide with interest, his great mouth watering. The hungry jackal remained hidden in the trees.

It was the rainy season and time to plant the corn. Clouds massed in the sky. Torrents of rain fell on the dusty earth. From early morning until late at night, the farmer toiled in his field, planting the corn, thinking only of his hen and chickens at home alone.

One day when the farmer was at work in his field, the jackal ran from the woods straight to the farmer's chicken coop, where he seized one of his chickens. That evening the farmer returned home too tired to count his chickens, as he usually did. Instead, he ate his simple meal and went to sleep.

The next day, after the farmer had gone to work in his field, the cunning jackal leaped from the woods and grabbed another chicken. Day after day, the jackal stole from the farmer, and the farmer, coming home late in the evening, was too tired to notice that his chickens were disappearing.

One evening, the farmer realized there was far less noise coming from his chicken coop than ever before. He went to have a look. You can imagine his surprise when he discovered only four chickens where once there had been twelve. "And they are the scrawniest!" exclaimed the farmer. "This must be the jackal's work." The next morning the farmer stayed home and lay in wait for the jackal.

As usual, the jackal, thinking the farmer was at work in his field, jumped from behind a bush and grabbed another chicken. This time the farmer was ready for him. He pounced on the jackal and held his leg, quickly fastening a rope around the animal's neck. He was about to hang him, when the jackal cried out, "Spare me! I will help you some day."

Reluctantly, the farmer gave in to the jackal's pleas and put the rope away. But he made the animal promise never to steal from him again.

Soon after, a terrible thing happened to the farmer. A rich landlord in the village tried to take away his field. The landlord came before the *panchayat*, offering bribes and false proof that the field belonged to him. When the jackal heard the landlord's wicked plan, he thought, "Now is the time to help the farmer."

Immediately he dug a tunnel from his lair to the place of the panchayat. Just as the old men were about to pronounce judgment in favor of the landlord, the jackal spoke from within the tunnel, his deep voice echoing. "I am the goddess of Earth," the jackal intoned. "You have angered me by taking what is not yours. Restore the field to the farmer."

The elders of the panchayat were terrified, the landlord quickly gave up his claim, and the field was returned to the farmer. The jackal, satisfied with his work, was feeling very hungry. He emerged from the tunnel and, without thinking, ran straight to the farmer's coop. He was about to pounce on another chicken when the farmer came home.

"Ah ha!" the farmer shouted. "You won't get off this time." He held the jackal to the ground, saying, "You'll steal no more chickens from me."

"My friend, did you not hear the voice from within the earth?" the jackal pleaded. "It was mine. It was I who saved your land, and I can do even more. Would you like the princess for your wife?" The farmer laughed out loud at the jackal's silliness.

"The princess for my wife, a castle over my head, and fields as far as the eye can see!" the farmer joked. But he let the jackal go, warning that the next time would be his last.

---

panchayat—a traditional court attended by five elders of the community

"You won't be sorry," called the jackal, as he headed for the palace. The jackal went straight before the king and proposed a marriage between the princess and a prince from a far-off land.

"The prince's wealth is enormous," the jackal boasted. "The marriage procession will stretch for miles." "Let it be," said the king, agreeing to the marriage.

The next day the jackal went to the farmer and told him he had to get ready for his wedding and to arrange for a bandmaster. The farmer just threw back his head and laughed, but the jackal insisted. "Such silliness!" said the farmer, going off to dress in his finest white shirt and his gayest *rungi chungi topi*.

Soon all was ready, and the farmer, the bandmaster, and the jackal all set off for the king's palace. They walked and walked until they came to a river that was flowing on the outskirts of the city. Along the banks of the river, bamboo bushes grew. Without saying a word, the jackal set fire to the bushes. The crackling of their burning echoed far and wide.

The jackal then ordered the bandmaster to blow on his *narsinga*. The sound was like an elephant trumpeting. The people in the city, hearing the hustle and bustle from the other side of the river, believed a marriage procession was coming toward them.

At sundown, the farmer, the bandmaster, and the jackal reached the palace and went before the king. "Where is the marriage procession that stretches for miles?" demanded the king. "Have you lied to me?" The jackal bowed low and spoke with respect.

"Your majesty, we did bring a marriage procession that had no end, but as we were crossing the river, a sudden flood came up and all of our people were carried away. Only the bridegroom, the bandmaster, and I somehow managed to swim across."

"We heard the shrill notes of the narsinga in the distance," the king replied, "and the crackling of the *badai*. Then he said, "We are very sorry for what has happened to your people. Now I am ready to give my daughter to your prince and half of my kingdom as well."

---

rungi chungi topi—a colorfully striped cap

narsinga—a long trumpet-like instrument

badai—fireworks

So on a fortunate day, the marriage ceremony took place, the princess pleased with her hearty prince, who smiled to himself at how such silliness had changed his luck. The farmer and the princess lived happily together with the jackal close beside, enjoying a fresh, plump chicken every day. 🐾

Two Brothers

Once in a certain village lived two brothers, one much older than the other. When the younger was still a child, their father died, and the eldest inherited all of his property—his fields and his house, his yak and his chickens. He shared none of these with his younger brother. Instead he beat him and made him do all the work.

Life was hard for the younger brother, and each year it grew worse. Finally, when the days became too difficult for him to bear, he decided to run away. One morning, in the dark before dawn, he crept quietly from the house, leaving his older brother snoring in the bed.

The younger brother walked for days until he came to a dense forest. At the edge of the forest stood an abandoned *dharmsala*, its boards rotting, its top floor leaning out over a cliff. He decided to rest there for the night and climbed the rickety stairs to the garret floor. There he lay down and immediately fell asleep.

As he slept, the serpent *Naga* slithered onto the ground floor of the dharmsala and coiled himself in a corner. Soon after, a mouse entered, then a tiger, then a mountain goblin. It was midnight on the Night of the New Moon and, as was their custom, the four creatures had come to sleep in the dharmsala. This night, before closing their eyes, they talked for a while, each creature bragging in his turn.

The mouse spoke first. "Friends, there is no one as happy as I! My wives and I have more food than we can eat because of what we steal from the king's granary."

---

dharmsala—inn

Naga—serpent linked with obscure forces of the underworld which guards the treasures hidden in the womb of the earth and the springs that give it life

The tiger spoke next, twirling his whiskers. "Ah ha! I am far happier than you. As I roam the forest, all the animals tremble before me. For my dinner, I prowl the king's cattle farm and take my pick of his fattest heifers."

The Naga, listening quietly to the boasts of his friends, cried out, "Poor fellows! You think you are fortunate because you eat the king's grain and devour his heifers? Why, I am luckier than you, for I lie at the bottom of a pond on a bed of precious jewels, which I have taken, one by one, from the royal treasury."

When the serpent had finished, the goblin laughed out loud. "None of you have the least idea what happiness is," he said. "You all know that the king has a severe pain in one of his eyes and that to ease this pain, the *jhankri* offers a fresh chicken and a well-cooked rice pudding to the jungle goddess every day. Every day I feast on that. Little does the king know that to be cured he must sacrifice a large black ram and worship the jungle goddess with a mixture of rice grains, yogurt, and vermilion. Only then will his pain go away."

It grew later on the Night of the New Moon, and one by one the creatures fell asleep. The youth on the garret floor above had been awakened by their voices and listened carefully to their every word. Now he knew that the king was in trouble and that he could help him.

At dawn a cock in a nearby village crowed. The four creatures awoke and went on their way. As the sun climbed higher in the sky, the young man arose, remembering clearly all he had heard from the night before. He descended the rickety steps of the dharmsala and ran straight to the palace, where he introduced himself at the gates as a healer and soothsayer. The guardsmen brought him before the king, who listened to him with interest.

The younger brother said, "The grain in your granary gets lower every day, your cattle are disappearing, and your precious jewels vanishing. Worst of all, you are suffering from a severe pain in your eye." The king was astounded at what the young man knew. "If you wish to regain your good fortune," the youth went on, "you must do as I tell you."

---

jhankri—witch doctor or traditional healer

"I will do whatever you ask," said the king, "if only you will rid me of my troubles. I am ready to offer my daughter in marriage and half of my kingdom."

"Your Majesty, I am a poor man, but I need no reward. I only wish to rid you of your suffering." The king felt hopeful.

Late that night, the youth went to the royal granary and blocked up all of the holes. Then he ran to the king's cattle farm and built a strong wall around it, higher than any tiger could leap. Just before dawn, he went to the pond and drained it of all its water. At the bottom he found the king's precious jewels, which he brought back to the palace.

In the morning, the young man asked the king for a large, black ram and some rice grains mixed with yogurt and vermilion powder. Gladly, the king gave him what he asked. Then the young man led the ram to a crossroads and, scattering the rice mixture about, performed the ritual before a sacrifice. He then sacrificed the ram and offered its blood to the jungle goddess.

When the younger brother returned to the palace, everyone ran out to greet him. They couldn't believe what had happened. The pain in the king's eye was gone, his grain and cattle remained untouched, and his jewels rested safely in the royal treasury.

The king was happier than he'd been in a long while and rewarded the young man with half of his kingdom. The princess, standing at her father's side, offered her hand to the younger brother. Now the young man's fame spread throughout the land. His older brother heard the news and set out for the capital to see for himself.

When he arrived in the city, he discovered that his younger brother was indeed prince. He hurried to the palace to see him. "How have you become so fortunate?" the older brother asked.

The younger brother was honest and told his brother everything, exactly as it had happened.

The older brother's heart was filled with envy. He wanted to become even richer and more powerful than his younger brother, so he decided to do exactly what his brother had done.

On the next Night of the New Moon, the older brother went to the dharmsala and climbed the rickety stairs to the garret floor. Immediately he fell asleep. At midnight the four friends came together again. This time they did not brag.

The mouse spoke first. "Friends, I am now the most unfortunate of creatures. The holes of the granary are sealed. My wives and I have eaten nothing for days."

The tiger, the Naga, and the goblin each told of their misery, all suspecting that on the last Night of the New Moon, someone had overheard their conversation and gone to tell the king.

"Let us go upstairs," said the mouse. "We may catch someone hiding." Just as they suspected, they saw a man sleeping on the garret floor. The creatures took him to be the spy and the cause of their misfortune. The mouse bit him on the heel, the tiger began to roar, and the Naga slithered around the man's waist, squeezing tight. Then the goblin jumped on his shoulders and began to pluck at his hair.

The older brother leapt up in pain and terror and ran down the rickety steps of the dharmsala. He was never to be seen or heard of again. But the younger brother, prince of far and wide, lived happily all of his days, the lovely princess at his side. 🐚

The River Kamala

Story Note: *The River Kamala is sacred, as are all Nepalese rivers, and considered a source of life. The people of Nepal worship their rivers and do not directly befoul them.*

Long ago there lived a *Brahmin* who owned a slave girl named Kamala. Now this Brahmin wanted to make a pilgrimage to India to the holy River Ganges, the holiest of all rivers. His slave girl asked if she too could send an offering. Since she was a slave and owned no property, she asked her mistress for help. The Brahmin's wife agreed and gave Kamala a handful of radish leaves from the garden.

Kamala handed the raddish leaves to the Brahmin, saying, "Oh, master, I wish to make an offering of these green leaves to the holy River Ganges. Please carry them with you and offer them to the river."

The Brahmin said to Kamala, "Foolish girl, you would be better off with food or flowers."

"Oh, master," Kamala sighed, "I would like to make an offering of food or flowers, but I cannot afford it." Though Kamala's offering was poor, the Brahmin took it anyway, promising he would give it to the river. Then he left on his pilgrimage.

Fifteen days later, the Brahmin reached the River Ganges. How great was his joy when he bathed his body in its holy waters and worshipped it with his offerings. The following day he started for home, but to his surprise he discovered that at the end of the day he was in the same place from which he had started. The next day he set off again, but by the end of the day he was back where he had begun. So it happened on the third day. Now the Brahmin was exhausted and did not understand these strange occurrences.

Brahmin—a member of the highest order in the Hindu caste system

On the fourth day he was about to set off, when he felt in his pocket the dried raddish leaves the slave girl had given him. "Oh, dear," said the Brahmin, "I have forgotten to give Kamala's offering." With that, he walked toward the river and threw in the dried raddish leaves. To his surprise, a human form emerged from the water, holding the leaves in her hand.

"Who are you, oh goddess?" asked the Brahmin in surprise.

The goddess looked at the dried raddish leaves and, with tears in her eyes, said, "I am the River Ganges, sister of your slave girl Kamala. She is the youngest of my sisters and my most beloved. In a former life, she took a loan from you and failed to repay it, so in this life she is destined to be your slave girl. Now she has worked long enough to repay you. Please let her go."

The Brahmin, feeling very sorry he had taken a goddess as his slave, hurried home to release her. As he entered his village, he saw Kamala returning from the water tap. "Holy goddess Kamala!" the Brahmin called out. Kamala turned to see who had called her "goddess." When she saw it was her master, she vanished into air.

The Brahmin hurried to the spot where Kamala had been but saw only a water pot tilted on its side, the water flowing out. Day after day, the water flowed at this spot and was called the holy *River Kamala*, which flowed into the Ganges, the most sacred of all rivers.

To this day one may see a spring flowing out of a pitcher-like rock. The people of the area worship this spring, saying that Kamala is repaying her debt by providing water for them to drink and to irrigate the valley. ❦

River Kamala—in eastern Nepal between the Mahabharat Range and the Siwalik Mountains

From the Mango Tree

Long ago, in a certain country, there lived a king who had seven queens. But for all of his wives, he had no children. One day when the king was out walking, he stopped to rest on a *chautara* where sat a *sanyasi*, an old religious man. "Oh, *Mahatma*! I am so unlucky," cried the king to the sanyasi. "Peace and plenty reach to the farthest corners of my kingdom."

"That does not sound like ill luck to me," the sanyasi said.

The king went on. "But I am getting old and I have no children. What good is so much wealth and glory when there are none to inherit it?" The king began to weep.

Now the sanyasi was no ordinary man. He could make possible the impossible. He took pity on the king and said, "I understand your trouble. Take this magic staff and when you come to a fruit tree, hurl it up into its branches. Do this only once, then gather the fruit that has fallen and bring it to your queens. When they have eaten, one of them will bear you children."

The king then thanked the sanyasi and went on his way. He soon came to a mango tree heavy with fruit. Eagerly he took the staff in his right hand and, with all of his might, flung it up into the tree's branches. Six ripe mangos fell. "I have seven queens," said the king, "but I must be satisfied with six mangos." He returned to the palace and went straight to the eldest queen.

---

chautara—a low stone wall

sanyasi—a holy man

Mahatma—Holy One

"Share these fruits with all of my queens," the king ordered, handing her the mangos. The king left and the eldest queen gathered all of the queens to her, all but the youngest. "We will eat these fruits ourselves," said the eldest queen. "Why should we share them with the youngest queen? She is the king's favorite and does not share his love with us."

The queens agreed and quickly fell to eating the fruit, not knowing its secret. When the youngest queen heard that the king had brought fruit for all of his queens, she ran to him, asking her share. The king, realizing what his wives had done, was filled with sadness.

Nevertheless, he told the youngest queen the secret of the fruit. She ran quickly and gathered the pits of the mangos the others had eaten. Then, praying for a child, she ate whatever fruit still clung to them.

Soon after, to everyone's surprise, the youngest queen grew big and round. The king was beside himself with joy. The other queens pretended to delight in his happiness, but they were consumed with jealousy. When the time came for the baby to be born, the six queens gathered around the youngest queen, ordering her maidservants from the room. Then they watched as the youngest queen gave birth to twins, a boy and a girl. Exhausted from her labor, the young queen fell asleep without ever seeing her children.

The wicked queens grabbed the newborn babies, wrapped them in rags, and threw them from the palace window. The tiny infants landed in a prickly nettle bush. The queens then brought a *musli* and a broom and placed them beside the sleeping mother.

When the youngest queen awoke, she asked, "Where are my babies?"

"Here they are," said the queens, handing her the musli and the broom. The youngest queen could not believe her eyes. She turned her head aside, tears trickling down her cheeks.

When the king heard that his youngest queen had given birth to a broom and a musli, he howled with grief and anger and immediately made the youngest queen the servant of the others. He vowed never to look at her.

---

musli—a pestle used in grinding grain

Meanwhile, a poor woman passing outside the palace heard the cries of the babies in the nettle bush. She lifted the little ones out of the stinging branches and brought them to her home. There she nursed them and cared for them as though they were her own. The years passed and the tiny infants grew to be beautiful children. Every day they played by the palace well.

One day a queen passing by the well saw the children and, struck by their beauty and pleasant ways, approached them, asking, "Who are your parents?"

"Our mother carries water to the palace," the children replied.

"And your father?" asked the queen. The children could not answer.

The queen said, "Find out the name of your father and tell me tomorrow at this very spot." That evening the children told their guardian what the queen had said. The poor woman knew she must now tell the children their story.

"Dear ones, I am not your mother," she said. "I found you as babies in a stinging nettle bush beside the palace. I brought you here and raised you as though you were my own. I cannot tell who your parents are because I do not know."

The next day, when the queen approached the children by the palace well, the boy and girl told her all that their guardian had told them. At once, the queen knew that these were the children they had thrown from the palace window long ago. She ran to tell the others. The eldest queen said, "We must do away with these children immediately. No one must discover our deed." That night clouds covered the moon. The six queens left the palace and went to the well, where they dug a deep pit.

The following day, while the children were at play, the queens crept up behind them and pushed them into the pit. Then quickly they shoveled dirt in over them. The days passed and at the place where the children were buried, two large flowering trees grew up bearing beautiful, sweet-smelling blossoms.

One afternoon the eldest queen, passing by the trees, was amazed by their lovely flowers. "How I would love to wear a blossom in my hair," she said. But as she reached for a flower, the branch sprang away. She could touch only the branches without flowers. The queen was puzzled. In the same way, the other queens, drawn to the beauty of the trees, each tried to pluck a flower, but they could reach only the branches that bore no flowers.

One day, the youngest queen, passing by the blossoming trees, was captured by their beauty and sweet aroma. Looking up into their branches, she cried, "Beautiful flowers, how I would love to plait your petals in my hair. Still the king would not notice me." As she spoke, a flowering branch bent low. Gratefully, the youngest queen plucked a blossom.

When the other queens saw the flower in the youngest queen's hair, they were filled with envy and tried to snatch it away. The king, hearing the commotion, came running. Immediately he was captivated by the flower's beauty and sweet aroma. "Where is the tree that bore this blossom?" the king asked.

The youngest queen was too frightened to speak. The other queens told him. The king hurried from the palace to the place of the flowering trees, his six queens following after. When he arrived at the spot, the king stretched out his hand to pluck a flower, and a branch laden with blossoms bent to his reach. At this, the queens rushed forward, each trying to grab a flower for herself, but the branch swung quickly away.

The king was amazed. Why did the trees bow low to him and spring away from his queens? He commanded his servants to dig up the ground around the trees to discover the answer. In a short time, the servants unearthed two children, who miraculously, were still alive. The king could not believe his eyes. "Who has done this horrible deed?" he asked. "Tell me, dear children."

The children told the king their story, how a poor woman had found them in a nettle bush beside the palace and raised them with loving kindness. One day they were snatched from their play and buried. They had stayed alive by breathing through gaps in the earth and sucking the roots of trees.

The king then sent for the woman who had been their guardian and listened to her story. Then he gathered all of his councilors and ministers to try to discover who were the parents of these children. "We must bring every young woman in the kingdom before them," the king declared. "Whoever weeps at the sight of them, we will know to be their mother."

That day all the young women in the kingdom were brought before the children. Not one wept. The six queens, too, were brought forward, but their eyes remained dry.

The youngest queen was the only woman in the kingdom who had not come before the children. The king ordered his guards to look for her, but, try as they might, they could not find her. The king then went in search of her himself and found her imprisoned in the palace dungeon. "Who has done this deed?" the king asked the young queen.

"Your six queens," she replied.

The king removed her shackles and brought her to the place where the children were standing. As soon as the young queen saw the girl and the boy, her eyes filled with tears. Now everyone knew the youngest queen was their mother. But the king had suspected it all along. He turned to the other queens and, in a voice filled with rage, asked, "What have you done?" The queens trembled before him.

"Speak!" roared the king, and the six queens confessed their evil deeds. The king was furious and banished the wicked queens from his kingdom. Then he brought the youngest queen to his side to share in the joy of their children. And he brought the old woman who had rescued and raised the infants to the palace, as well.

Now the king and the queen's joy was complete as the sounds of children's laughter rang throughout the palace halls. 🖤

Death Invisible

Story Note: *This story chronicles the origin of alcohol, brought to earth by the goddess Sumnima to counter the wiles of men and to cause them to reveal themselves. It is told as an admonition against alcohol: to take it is to lose a lot.*

In ancient times, so it is told, Death was quite visible and took pity on his unsuspecting victims. That is, until a blacksmith tricked him. Then *Lord Paruhang* made Death invisible. Here's how the story is told.

For thousands of years, Death worked without incident, taking away each person whose time it was to die. One day, Death approached a blacksmith's wife who had just given birth to a son. Her husband quickly intervened. "Death," the husband pleaded, "you must reconsider. Please give my wife at least one or two more years so she may nurse our young son."

"My dear fellow," said Death, "I cannot help you." He ushered the blacksmith's wife out the door. Now it fell to the blacksmith to look after his new baby alone.

The following year, Death came again. "My good fellow," Death said to the blacksmith. "It is your time to go." The blacksmith fell at Death's feet, crying, "Oh, lord, I have no care for my own life. It is the life of my son that troubles me. He is so tiny. If I die, who will look after him? Please reconsider."

"You know that I can't," said Death.

"Then take us both together, please, both me and my son."

"No, dear fellow," Death replied. "You must understand I cannot take just anyone. Your son has sixty more years yet to live." "How could that possibly be," asked the blacksmith, "when there will be no one here to feed him or look after him? How can you be certain he will live that long? Please be sure of this."

Lord Paruhang—Lord Shiva, to the Kirati people of Nepal

Death thought to himself, "The blacksmith has a point." So he checked his book of who shall live and who shall die and saw that, indeed, the child was destined to live sixty years. Now Death was impatient to end the discussion. "Your child will live sixty more years. How, I do not know. My job is to take you now. Let us go." Death began dragging the blacksmith out the door, but the baby fell from his father's lap and cried loudly.

Tears streamed down the blacksmith's cheeks. "How can you take me while my child lies helpless on the floor? Do you not have a heart?"

Death stopped to reconsider and finally said, "I will give you one more year to care for your child."

The following year, Death came again. This time the blacksmith said, "Look at my baby. See how he wobbles when he walks. How can you leave him like this? Wait at least until he learns to become a blacksmith. Then he can earn his bread when I die."

The two haggled back and forth, until Death, moved by the blacksmith's argument, said, "Very well, I will wait until the boy turns sixteen. By then he should have learned the blacksmith's trade." "Thank you, my lord," said the blacksmith. "You are truly a great one."

Now the blacksmith was not only a persuasive fellow, he was cunning, as well, and he began to devise a plan to entrap Death.

The years passed and the blacksmith's son helped him with all of his work. The blacksmith had more time to work on his scheme.

At the end of fourteen years, the blacksmith had finished. His work looked like a huge mass of chains. Nobody knew what it was, not even his son.

On the day Death returned, the boy was not there. "Are you ready now, blacksmith?" asked Death. "By this time you must have trained your son well." The blacksmith pretended to be happy to see him. "Yes, lord, I am absolutely ready to go with you. My son has great skill. In fact, before I leave this world, I would like to show you his work. Please come with me."

Death followed the blacksmith inside the mass of chains. "His creation is indeed beautiful," said Death, "but I do not understand it."

"You will know when we reach the center," said the blacksmith. "You should be proud that the boy to whom you gave life has completed such a work."

The blacksmith and Death passed through seven chambers until they reached the center. The blacksmith then turned to Death and said, "Please be seated. I am going to show you how all of this works."

Death sat in the place that the blacksmith showed him, suspecting nothing. Suddenly the blacksmith ran from the mass of chains, locking all seven chambers behind him. Death was entrapped.

Immediately the blacksmith left the house and went out into the village, acting as though nothing had happened. He told no one what he had done, not even his son.

Since Death could not come out, no one died for years. The world became quite crowded, and life was uncomfortable. Lord Paruhang was worried. He thought Death was lost. He and his wife, the Goddess Sumnima, went out in search of him the world over. But Death was nowhere to be found.

One day Sumnima said, "Lord, I think Death has disappeared because of the mischief of some human beings. I have a plan to rescue him." Lord Paruhang allowed her to work in her own way.

Sumnima went down to earth in the form of a lady and immediately began cooking millet, mixing it with *marcha*, herbs that aid in fermentation. She put the mixture aside and covered it tightly. After four days, she uncovered the pot and began talking to the fermented liquid.

"Listen to me, *jaand*, your job is to speak the mind of the people as you go into their bodies." Sumnima then went off to a village to try to sell the jaand. She sat at a crossroad, and many people came to her. They drank the jaand and became quite drunk. Now, since it is known that drunkards talk a lot, Sumnima listened to everyone.

One day a group of smiths came to drink, the blacksmith among them. They too became quite drunk, and one of them moaned, "Oh, I'm so horribly drunk. I feel I am going to die." The blacksmith spoke up quickly. "Don't worry, you will not die, for I have entrapped Death. Be sure you tell no one. It is a deep secret."

_____

jaand—a local beer made of either millet, rice, wheat, or maize

Sumnima heard the blacksmith talking loudly in his drunken state and quickly left the place where she was sitting. She ran to the blacksmith's house and found Death locked in the chamber. She set him free and brought him before Lord Paruhang. Lord Paruhang was very angry.

"From this day on," he told Death, "you will have no feelings, no sentiments, no emotions. And you will be invisible to all human beings, unable to communicate with them." From that day on, Death has been both silent and invisible, and he pities no one. 🍎

The Uttis Tree

Thousands of years ago in the Himalayan mountains of Nepal, it was the custom for trees to marry. These marriages were arranged by *pipal* trees, who, because of their great height, could see to the farthest reaches of the forest.

One spring day, a matchmaking pipal was out looking for trees to join in marriage when he spied a full-blooming, red *laligurans*. Astonished by her beauty and brilliance, he called to Bandevi, the goddess of the forest. "Bandevi, do you see the crimson laligurans on the other side of the hill? Is she not beautiful beyond description? May I have your permission to find her a husband?"

The goddess Bandevi agreed and the pipal began his search, stretching his branches here and there, to the farthest corners of the forest. Suddenly he spied a tall, full-crowned evergreen *uttis* tree. He bent toward the uttis and said, "I have a magnificent wife for you. The splendid laligurans fills the eyes and hearts of all who behold her."

The uttis sniffed and held his handsome body even taller. "*I* will choose whom I will marry," the uttis said. "First I must see this laligurans. Then I will decide."

The pipal, annoyed at the arrogant pride of the uttis, replied, "I am busy just now and cannot arrange a meeting until midwinter." With that, the pipal gathered in his branches and looked away.

---

pipal—a banyan tree

laligurans—rhododendron, the national flower of Nepal

uttis—evergreen that grows primarily at the bottom of cliffs and where there have been landslides

All that spring and into the summer the trees lengthened their limbs, putting forth new leaves. In the fall many of the trees lost their greenery. In winter, the snow deep on the ground, the trees stood bare against the sky. But the uttis, strong and hearty, remained green and handsome as ever.

The pipal, true to his word, arranged a meeting between the uttis and the laligurans. The day of the meeting the uttis was in a jovial mood. He strode across the snow toward the laligurans. As he drew nearer, he could see the tips of her branches over the hill and his pace slowed. Then he stopped and stared. Was this the splendid laligurans the pipal had praised so loudly? He could not believe his eyes. Why, she was nothing but a crooked skeleton, her flowers gone, her foliage limp and curled.

The uttis, thinking the pipal had deceived him, was enraged. He turned his back and stomped off. The pipal begged him to look again, but the uttis remained deaf to his pleas. The laligurans stood alone, shivering in the winter wind.

Time passed, and in the spring the beauty of the laligurans returned. Again all the trees of the forest were dazzled by her blossoms. Once again the pipal called on the uttis to arrange a meeting with the laligurans. So persuasive was he that the uttis agreed to have another look. "You'd better not deceive me this time," the uttis cautioned.

Indeed! This time the uttis was so overwhelmed by the beauty of the laligurans he fell deeply in love with her. Gently he swept his branches to her trunk and in a soft, pleading voice asked, "Will you marry me?" But the laligurans, whose heart had been bruised in the winter, refused.

The uttis was struck dumb. He turned to the pipal and begged him to speak on his behalf, to use all of his powers of persuasion to show the laligurans how tall and proud he was, how he remained ever green. But the laligurans had made up her mind and would not change it.

The uttis, desperate and confused, stumbled over the side of a cliff and landed in a ravine, his roots clasping the jagged rocks. The trees of the mountain slopes and forests looked down at the uttis clinging to the rocks and felt afraid.

Bandevi, sensing their fear, outlawed the custom of marriage between the trees. And from that day on, the matchmaking pipal vowed he would never be a matchmaker again. But the sadness of the uttis lives on. To this very day, he grows only where he fell, in the ravines and deep mountain gullies of Nepal. 🍏

Princess Naulakha

Once in a certain country lived a king who had six sons and one beautiful daughter. The princess was named Naulakha. She was the youngest and much beloved by her brothers. The years passed, and when the old king died, his eldest son took the throne.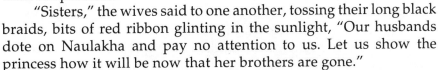

Naulakha was by now a woman of grace, with long dark hair and eyes that were large and luminous. Her brothers saw that she should soon be married, so they set off to find her a husband. Their wives, an ill-natured, jealous lot, were left alone in the palace with the princess.

"Sisters," the wives said to one another, tossing their long black braids, bits of red ribbon glinting in the sunlight, "Our husbands dote on Naulakha and pay no attention to us. Let us show the princess how it will be now that her brothers are gone."

The wives forced Naulakha to do all the work of the palace and barely gave her enough to eat. They took away all of her beautiful *saris* and tossed her their old tattered ones to wear instead. The princess grew sad, but there was no one to comfort her. Quietly she did as she was told and ate the little she was given.

One day the wives called to Naulakha and ordered her to fetch a bundle of firewood from the forest. But they didn't give her so much as a *namlo* to tie it with. "You must do this task," they told her, "before you return home."

Heavyhearted, Naulakha set off for the forest to collect the wood. She gathered a pile of twigs and branches, then looked about for something to tie them with, but she could find nothing. Tired and afraid, she sat down to rest. A python hanging from a nearby tree spied her. "Beautiful maiden," he said, "what has befallen you?"

---

sari—Nepalese dress

namlo—strap

The princess told him her story, and the large snake took pity on her. He slithered down the tree and coiled himself around the bundle of firewood like a namlo. The princess then picked up the bundle and carried it home.

When Naulakha appeared in the palace with the firewood neatly tied, the evil-hearted wives could not believe their eyes. Quickly they ordered her to another task, this time to bring water from a near-empty well. Naulakha went to the well, but hard as she tried, she could not reach the low water at the bottom. She called out in frustration, "If I cannot do this task, I will surely be banished."

Hearing her words, the water god at the bottom of the well caused the water to swell to the top. The princess then filled her brass pitcher and hurried home.

The evil-hearted wives could not believe Naulakha had drawn water from a near-empty well. They assigned her to another task, this time to peel the husks off every grain of rice in a large sack, using only her fingernails. Naulakha brought the sack to a field and began to work. After many hours, she found she had peeled only a tiny portion of the rice grains. She sighed deeply.

The king of the birds, hearing her sigh, ordered his subjects, great and small, to the job. In an instant, the birds had peeled the husks off every grain of rice.

The princess went home, the sack of peeled rice at her side. Her brothers' wives were surprised to see she had finished the task so quickly. They could not believe she had done exactly as they told her, so they sat down to count the grains, one by one. To their great glee, they discovered that, indeed, one grain of rice was missing. They ordered Naulakha to find the missing grain at once.

Naulakha returned to the king of the birds and told him her plight. Immediately the king ordered a search for the lost grain. A bluejay found it stuck on the beak of a young crow. Naulakha went home with the lost grain and gave it to her sisters-in-law.

The hardhearted wives were amazed. Each time they had given Naulakha a difficult task, she had completed it. Now they tried to think of something utterly impossible. They huddled together, whispering and scheming, until finally they decided on the most difficult task of all. They gave Naulakha a black blanket and ordered her to wash it until it turned white. She was not to return home until the job was done.

The obedient princess brought the blanket to a nearby stream and began washing it. Day after day, she sat by the stream, washing the blanket, beating it with stones, swirling it in the rushing water. But the blanket remained as black as ever.

Days became months and still Naulakha knelt by the stream, washing the blanket. Passersby on their way to the temple called out, *"Namaste!"* But the princess was too tired to answer.

Day after day, she ate the leaves and the roots of plants, for the cruel wives barely fed her. Each day she grew thinner. Her face, once so full and lustrous, was now withered and gray. One chilly day, as the princess sat by the stream, washing the blanket, a group of travelers passed by. Moved by the sight of her, they asked, "Who are you, sister?"

Naulakha looked up and saw that the travelers were her brothers. In a weak and trembling voice, she told them who she was and all that had happened. The princes could not bear to hear their sister's story. "Dear Naulakha!" they cried. "Our wives have made you suffer. Now they will be made to suffer more than you." They lifted her frail body from the bank of the stream and carried her home.

When the wives saw their husbands coming, they ran out to greet them, offering food and fresh flowers. Telling lie after lie, they pretended to be greatly concerned about Naulakha's dwindling health.

The princes, unable to tolerate their wives' hypocrisies, were about to put the women to death, when Naulakha came before them, pleading for mercy on their behalf. Reluctantly the brothers agreed to spare the women's lives but banished them from the kingdom forever.

Once again Princess Naulakha walked with grace and again dressed in flowing saris. A fine prince had been found and soon they were married. The princess was now as happy as before. Her love for her brothers and theirs for her remained strong and faithful all of their days. ❦

Namaste!—Greetings!

King Silly and Minister Sloppy

Story Note: *According to certain theories, this story comes from the life of one Mukundasen, King of Palpa in western Nepal who, renowned for his wisdom and saintliness, conquered the village of Vijayapore.*

Long ago, King Silly and his trusted advisor Minister Sloppy ruled over Vijayapore, a village in eastern Nepal. Vijayapore was unique among the villages of the country, because in its central square, goods of the same color were sold for the same price. For example, rice, milk, silver, cotton, and flour, all white, sold for one price and brass, gold, and turmeric, all yellow, sold for another.

Now King Silly and Minister Sloppy introduced another law, not quite as logical as the first, which said that *saints* were to be punished by hanging and thieves rewarded with the pleasure of resting in the cool, delicious shade. People from other parts of the country used to say that because of these ridiculous laws, a saint should never venture into Vijayapore.

One day, however, two wandering saints came to the village. They had heard that milk, rice and millet flour were all the same price and wanted to barter their cheap millet flour for some rice and milk to make a lovely rice pudding. However, the bartering took some time, and when they had finished, it had grown dark. The two saints were forced to spend the night in Vijayapore, though they knew it was dangerous.

The saints stayed in a cow-shade but could not sleep from worry about what might happen to them in this strange village. That very night, close to where the saints were resting, thieves broke into a house. The saints saw everything but were too frightened to call out.

---

saints—holy men

It so happened that while the thieves were breaking into the house, one of them banged his head on a low door. "Aieee!" cried the thief, rubbing his head. He was furious and went directly to the palace to tell the king what had happened to him. King Silly was very angry at the news of the low door and asked that the door be brought before him.

The owner of the house, on hearing the king's request, came to him, pleading on the door's behalf. "Oh, king, my door is innocent," the owner said. "It is the carpenter who made it who is at fault." The king then ordered his soldiers to bring him the carpenter. The carpenter too pleaded his innocence.

"My lord, it is not my fault," he said. "It is the fault of the timber supplier. His boards were so short I had to make the door low." The king then ordered his soldiers to bring him the timber supplier. The timber supplier came to the court, pleading his innocence.

"It was not my fault, great justice! In fact, there are no tall trees left in the forest. All have been cut down to build the royal palace."

Now King Silly and Minister Sloppy were in a dilemma. Here was a person whose head was hurt, but no one was responsible. How could this be? they wondered. Then one of the members of the king's court, Courtier Unfair, came forward.

"Oh king, I know who is responsible for this accident," said Courtier Unfair. "While the thieves were breaking into the house, two saints were in a nearby cow-shade taking shelter. They saw everything but did not warn the thief about the low door. So in my opinion, it is the saints who should be punished." The king was now very happy, as was his minister.

The king quickly ordered his soldiers to bring him the saints. "We must hang them immediately," said the king, feeling well pleased.

The saints came before the king, and the elder of the two bowed low, saying, "Oh great king of the world, we have heard you are just and wise. And we have heard you never make a mistake and never fail to do your duty. So we accept your punishment without question. But may I speak with my friend before I am hanged?"

There was a rule in Vijayapore stating that the last wish of the person who is about to be hanged must be granted. "Yes, you may speak with your friend," the king agreed.

After a few moments, however, the saints were arguing over who was to be hanged first. The king, the minister, and the courtiers were all very puzzled. Never had they seen anyone competing to die. "What is this nonsense?" scolded the king. "Why do you argue over who will hang first?"

"Oh, just king," said the elder saint. "Please give us your wise counsel. Since I am older than my friend, shouldn't I be hanged first?"

But the younger saint argued, "I am the younger, so I should have the first opportunity. What if a father and his young child are both very hungry, and they find a single grain of rice—who should have the chance to eat it?"

"Why, the child, of course," said the king.

"But oh, great justice," interrupted the elder saint. "Ours is not a case of hunger but a case of rights. Tell us then, king, if there is an opportunity, who has the right to become king—the junior or the senior?"

"Neither," said the king, "for *I* am king."

"But my lord," said the older saint, "this is not your story, it is our story. We are about to be hanged today in Vijayapore, and we know that whoever is hanged first, will be Vijayapore's king in a future life. The one who is hanged last will be minister. So tell us, who should be hanged first?"

"Ah!" said the king. "I recognize your cunning. I see that you two saints are conspiring to become the future king and minister of Vijayapore. There'll be none of that!"

"Soldiers!" called the king. "Take these saints to the border and see that they never return." As soon as he had spoken, the king hurried to the gallows and hung himself.

Then the minister announced, "There will be no other minister but I!" And he too hurried to the gallows. Courtier Unfair came forward in a rush. "It is plain I must remain a courtier in the next life." He ran to the gallows and hung himself.

So ended the ridiculous ways of the village of Vijayapore. The elder saint became king, the younger his minister, and the people were overjoyed to have reason restored. 🌱

Tuhuri and the She-Goat

Once in a certain village lived a motherless child named Tuhuri. Her father was kind to her, but her stepmother treated her cruelly and barely gave her enough to eat.

Tuhuri seemed never to complain. The young girl had a she-goat which her dying mother had passed on to her for a dowry. Every day Tuhuri took the goat deep into the forest, away from the eyes and ears of the villagers. There she fed it the crusts of dry bread her stepmother had thrown to her and poured out her grief. The she-goat listened, tears of sympathy flowing.

It happened that the she-goat had the power to produce food. Whenever she and Tuhuri were alone in the woods, the goat shook her body and tasty delicacies fell to the ground. The girl ate hungrily whatever had fallen, thanking her god for rewarding her with such a good friend. The stepmother saw that despite the stale crusts of bread Tuhuri was given, the girl remained healthy and strong. But her own children, who ate only the finest food, appeared skinny and pale. "How can this be?" the stepmother wondered. One day she bade her daughter follow Tuhuri to watch her carefully.

The stepmother's daughter went to Tuhuri and sweetly asked, "Won't you take me into the forest with you?" The kindhearted Tuhuri, suspecting nothing, agreed.

The two went deep into the forest. Then Tuhuri stopped and fed the she-goat some crusts of dry bread. When she asked the goat to conjure up some delicacies, the animal refused. Tuhuri began to cry and beg for food, her pleas so piteous the goat finally gave in. Reluctantly, the animal shook its body and several tasty morsels fell to the ground. The stepsister was amazed. Never had she seen such a wonder. She ate a few of the delicious tidbits and hid the rest in her clothing.

Tuhuri begged the girl not to tell her mother what she had just seen. The cunning stepsister assured her she wouldn't.

Dusk was fast approaching, and they hurried home. When they reached the hut, the stepsister went straight to her mother and, showing her the delicious delicacies, told her everything. The stepmother's eyes blazed with anger. She stamped her foot and shrieked, "I will kill that goat!" And she began to hatch a plan to destroy the animal.

The stepmother knew that since the goat was Tuhuri's only possession, the girl's father would not let her kill it that easily. She had to think of a way to deceive him. Suddenly she pretended to fall ill. Tossing and turning on her bed, she cried out as though in great pain. Her worried husband rushed to her side, asking what was the matter. "My stomach pains me so," the deceitful woman wailed.

The husband ran quickly to a neighbor, calling, "*Dai!* My wife has a great pain in her stomach. What must I do?" The neighbor, who had been secretly bribed by the wife, told the husband he must fry the liver of a she-goat in pure *ghee*, then feed it to his beloved. "Only this will make her well," the neighbor said.

Immediately the husband decided to kill the goat and make an offering to the angry god who was tormenting his wife. As soon as Tuhuri heard of her father's plan, she ran, in tears, to tell the goat. The unfortunate she-goat comforted her, saying, "Take heart and listen. When they give you my bones, carry them to the edge of the cornfield and bury them there." Soon after, the she-goat was killed.

The weeping girl took its bones to the cornfield and buried them in the corner, her tears wetting the newly-turned soil.

The days went by, and Tuhuri's stepmother continued to torment her. Whenever she could slip away, Tuhuri ran to the place where the goat was buried. There she sat weeping, her fresh tears falling to the ground.

After a time, Tuhuri noticed something strange happening. In the corner of the field where the bones were buried, shoots of pure gold were sprouting. Tuhuri could not believe her eyes. Feeling hungry, she plucked a few of the shoots and took them to the market to trade for food.

---

dai—elderly brother

ghee—butter

The shopkeepers were amazed when they saw Tuhuri bringing shoots of pure gold to the market. Day after day she brought them, and rumors began to fly from one corner of the village to the other. The stepmother, hearing the talk, began to watch the girl more closely. One day she followed her to the cornfield and discovered her secret. The next day the stepmother went alone to the spot where the shoots were growing and tried to pull one up. But she could not budge it.

News of the golden shoots reached the king, who set off to see for himself, trailing soldiers and courtiers behind him. When they reached the cornfield, the king saw the golden shoots growing in abundance. He had heard they were difficult to extract, so he ordered his strongest men to try it. But the shoots wouldn't budge.

The king then ordered his men to look for Tuhuri. They searched throughout the village, and finally found her sitting by the side of a stream, washing her stepmother's clothing. Quickly they brought her before the king.

The king saw at once that the girl had a kind and generous spirit and hoped in his heart they would marry. He spoke gently to her. "Kind maiden, won't you pull a shoot from the cornfield?"

Moved by the king's quiet ways, Tuhuri plucked a shoot as though it were as light as a dry stalk. She held it out to him, and the king accepted it. Then he asked her to marry. Tuhuri went to join him at the head of his caravan.

The sun rose in the sky, shining brilliantly on the king and his new queen. Tuhuri smiled at her good fortune, but in her heart she carried the sad memory of the she-goat all of her days.

The Cave of Halesi

Story Note: *Caves, like the rivers in Nepal, are considered sacred, for they were places of meditation for the saints, or holy men.*

Long ago, the demon Bhasmasur worshipped *Lord Mahadeva*, god of destruction. Lord Mahadeva was so pleased by the demon's worship that he appeared before him, saying, "What is it you want? Tell me, so I may fulfill your wish."

Bhasmasur was delighted and said to the god, "Oh Lord, grant me my wish. Let it be that whomever I touch turns to ash."

Now Mahadeva was easily flattered and quick to act. Without thinking, he fulfilled the demon's wish. "*Tathastu,*" he said. "Let it be." After a few moments, Bhasmasur asked, "Is my wish working?"

"Dear demon," said Mahadeva, "how can you ask such a question? Of course you have the power you requested."

"Oh, Lord," cried Bhasmasur, "how will I know unless I test it. Since there is no one here but you, may I place my hand on your head?"

"Fool!" cried Mahadeva, "then I will be turned to ash!"

"But, oh Lord!" said Bhasmasur, "how will I know if my wish works?"

With that, the demon stepped forward, his hand outstretched toward Mahadeva's head. Mahadeva, frightened, stepped back, and the demon moved forward. Mahadeva, realizing he had made a terrible mistake, tried to escape. He ran to his family in the mountains, but still the demon followed.

Cave of Halesi—a place of religious pilgrimage

Lord Mahadeva—another name for Lord Shiva

When Mahadeva arrived at *Mt. Halesi*, he dug a hole in the mountain to hide himself and his family, his wife Parvati and his son Ganesh. While he was digging the hole, his mount, the ox Basaha, stood fighting at the entrance of the cave to keep the demon away. But the ox was defeated, and the demon pushed his way downward.

Mahadeva heard the demon coming and began to dig another hole, this time tunneling upward toward the earth's surface. The demon was close behind, so Mahadeva dug another hole, this one going downward. In the bottom of the new hole he hid himself and his family.

Vishnu, the god of preservation, saw what was happening and came to earth in the form of a beautiful maiden. The maiden approached the demon, who was looking tired and sad. "Oh, great demon," she said, "why are you looking so sad?"

"My lady," said Bhasmasur, "Lord Mahadeva has cheated me. He granted me my wish but escaped before I could find out whether it worked." The maiden laughed out loud.

"Why are you laughing?" asked Bhasmasur.

"Because it is funny, of course," said the maiden. "Why do you have to find someone to test your wish. Why not try it on yourself?"

"How could I do that?" asked Bhasmasur.

"You could put your hand on your own head."

"Ah, what a fool I am," said Bhasmasur. "Why did I not think of that?" Laughing at his own foolishness, Bhasmasur said, "Oh lady, please be my witness and see if my wish works." Bhasmasur then put his hand on his own head and immediately was turned to ash.

Now today, if you go to Mt. Halesi in eastern Nepal, you will see the caves dug by Lord Mahadeva. One is called Basahathan, the place of Basaha who fought the demon. At its entrance is a boulder that looks like an ox. The second cave is called Mahadevathan, the place of Lord Mahadeva. On the floor of this cave are many stalagmites, which people say are the gods who came to visit Lord Mahadeva while he was in hiding. One stalagmite is the lord himself, two others, his wife and son. On the roof of the cave, stalactites drip lime water onto the stalagmites, which people say are offerings of milk from heaven for the visiting gods and goddesses.

About two miles away is a pile of black rocks, said to be the burnt relics of the demon Bhasmasur. So goes the story of the cave of Mt. Halesi. 🐚

Mt. Halesi—in the foothills of the Himalayas of eastern Nepal

The Three Rules

Once upon a time there lived a very wise king. He was so wise the rulers of other countries came to him for counsel. The king's son was also very wise and sat beside his father during all of his deliberations.

One day the king's son died, leaving a small child, Buddhivir. The son's wife was so overcome with sadness that she too died a few days later. Now Buddhivir was an orphan, and his grandparents, the king and queen, raised him with loving kindness.

The years passed and the king became quite ill. He knew he would soon die, so he called for his grandson Buddhivir, who was only twelve at the time. The young prince sat beside him, listening as he spoke, "My child, soon I will die. Before I go, I would like to leave you with three rules. These will make you successful in life. Always remember them: Make friends with well-bred people. Marry a girl from a well-bred family. Work for a well-bred king.

The king died, and the old queen named Buddhivir prince regent until the age of sixteen. When Buddhivir turned sixteen, the queen said to him, "Oh, my grandson, it is time you became king."

Young Buddhivir said, "Oh, grandmother, let me first explore the truth of the rules my grandfather told me."

"They are simple instructions, my child," said the old queen. "You need only remember them, and they will help you."

"But what happens if I do not remember them or if I neglect them?"

"Then you will fail in life."

"What does it mean to fail?" the young prince asked.

"I do not know," said his grandmother, "for your father and grandfather were so wise they never failed. Our country has never known failure."

"Grandmother, I want to be successful, but I must be prepared for failure. I must test my grandfather's rules."

"How will you test them?" asked the old queen.

"By experimenting."

"Oh no, my dear, that is too dangerous."

"Oh grandmother, do not worry. I will survive with the wisdom inherited from my father and my grandfather. Please do not stop me. You will only make me a coward and cast doubt on the good name of my forefathers."

"My child, let the tradition of bravery continue in this dynasty. I have no doubt you will succeed. Go and do honor to the names of your predecessors. Good luck."

Young King Buddhivir set off for a poor country where the king was known to be rude, tyrannical, and mean. He went straight before the court and introduced himself as a prince who had come to discover certain truths about life. He asked the king for a job so he could earn his bread while he experimented.

The king laughed and said, "What skills do you have? Princes are brought up to do nothing. You will probably only spoil things if I give you a job of any importance. Oh well, you can look after the peacock farm, but, mind you, if one of them dies, you will be killed." Buddhivir accepted the position and went off to tend the peacocks.

He soon wanted to test his grandfather's advice further, so he looked for someone to be his best friend, someone he could join in performing the ritual for becoming *mit*.

In Buddhivir's neighborhood there lived a tailor master, who was proud, greedy, illiterate, and selfish. In order to test his grandfather's rules, Buddhivir proposed a ritual friendship with him.

The tailor master agreed to the friendship only if Buddhivir would give him a diamond ring. Buddhivir said he would, then he asked for the tailor's help in finding him a wife. The tailor agreed only if he received a diamond necklace in addition. Buddhivir consented.

The next day the tailor introduced Buddhivir to a girl from his own family. The young man quickly saw that the girl was ill-bred.

Days passed and the people of the kingdom remained selfish, greedy, and mean. Now Buddhivir decided it was time to experiment more seriously. He went secretly to the market and bought a big chicken, which he killed and plucked. When he came home, he gave the chicken to his wife and said, "Now prepare a big feast." His wife was delighted and said, "What bird is this? Without any feathers, I cannot tell."

---

mit—male friends forever, almost a member of the family

"Shhh," cautioned Buddhivir. "Speak softly. It is a peacock from the king's farm. If you tell anyone, I shall be put to death."

"My goodness," said his wife. "It's been almost a year since I have eaten meat. Oh, beloved husband, you are so wise and good to steal a peacock from the king's farm. I myself have thought of it many times, but now you have done it. Thank goodness."

"Yes, my beloved wife, but don't tell a soul." That night the two feasted.

The next morning, Buddhivir's wife went to the watering place, picking her teeth. The wife of the tailor master came up to her, saying, "*Mitini*, what did you eat last night that you are picking your teeth?"

"Ah, it is a secret, but I must at least boast of my husband's bravery. I can say this to my own ritual friend, assured that it will not reach a third party."

"Oh, my mitini, trust me. I swear I will tell no other woman."

"Then give my your ear and I will whisper the truth."

Boasting of her husband's wisdom and bravery, Buddhivir's wife told her friend what they had eaten the night before. Her friend also praised Buddhivir's wisdom and bravery and vowed to speak of it to no other woman in the community. The moment the tailor master's wife arrived home, she scolded her husband for not being as wise as his mit.

"Oh, him!" said the tailor master. "He is a cheat!"

"Did he not give you the diamond ring and the necklace?"

"No. I won those for myself."

"I am so jealous that my mitini boasted of her husband's bravery," said the tailor master's wife. "I could not bear it."

"Don't be so agitated, my lady. I am going straight before the king and report to him that my mit has stolen his peacock."

"Oh, don't do that, for the king will surely kill your friend in punishment."

"Who cares?" said the tailor master. "The king will reward me for the information."

"You are right," said the tailor master's wife. "I did not think of that."

---

mitini—best female friend

"Now you see how smart I am, don't you?" asked the tailor master.

"And do you see how much smarter I am than my mitini?" his wife asked. "I swore to keep the matter secret and to tell no other woman in the community. But that way I was free to tell a man. If I were not so smart, you wouldn't have the opportunity to go before the king."

The next morning the tailor master went straight before the king and reported that Buddhivir had stolen a peacock. The king was furious and ordered that Buddhivir be hanged. When Buddhivir was brought before the king, he pleaded on his own behalf, "Oh, king, let one of your courtiers count the peacocks in your farm. If a single one is missing, I will hang myself."

Promptly the king sent one of his courtiers to count the peacocks, but he found none missing. When he reported this to the king, the king was furious and ordered the tailor master hung for a liar. The tailor master pleaded with the king, saying it was not his fault, but his wife's, who had lied to him. The king then ordered that his wife, too, be hanged.

When the tailor master's wife came before the king, she confessed it was her mitini, Buddhivir's wife, who had lied to her. The king then gave an order to hang Buddhivir's wife. When she appeared before the king, she accused her husband of lying. "He is the main criminal," she said, pointing her finger at him.

The king then put Buddhivir's name back on the list of those to be hanged.

When Buddhivir came before the king, he said, "Oh, king, why should anyone be hanged when there are no peacocks missing?"

Still the king was unsatisfied. He considered the root of all the trouble to be the foreigner standing before him, so he ordered his soldiers to throw Buddhivir out of the kingdom and to kill him if he returned. Further, he ordered his courtiers to remove the tongues of the two wives and the tailor master, since they had all lied.

Buddhivir's life was saved, and he understood why one should not deal with ill-bred people. He thought he should now try an experiment with well-bred people to more fully understand his grandfather's rules. He did not return to his country but went on to another, which was known to be prosperous, cultured, and civilized.

When he arrived at the court, he introduced himself as Prince Buddhivir and said he was on a quest to discover certain truths about life. He asked if the king would provide him with a job, so he could earn his bread as he experimented.

The king was happy to meet Buddhivir and said, "You appear to be a well-bred young man. Will you share with us whatever you learn from your experiment? Since you are the crown prince's age, I will employ you as his guardian."

Buddhivir gladly accepted the position and found the crown prince to be diligent and wise. The young man recognized Buddhivir's wisdom, as well, and, without hesitation, followed his advice. Since Buddhivir had helped his own grandfather govern his country, he was also able to help the crown prince.

Close to where Buddhivir lived was a humble businessman, polite, friendly, generous, and educated. Buddhivir wanted to have a ritual friendship with him as part of his experiment, so he performed the ritual for being mit.

The businessman was delighted with his new friendship and presented Buddhivir with diamond rings, a gold necklace, and a house to live in. Graciously Buddhivir accepted the presents, then asked his friend's help in finding him a wife. The businessman told Buddhivir of a friend who was a general in the military who had a splendid daughter.

"It will be a good match," he said. Buddhivir agreed and the businessman went off to arrange for the marriage ceremony.

Days passed and life went on pleasantly. But one day when Buddhivir and the crown prince were out hunting, Buddhivir asked the prince if he would help him perform a very serious experiment. "Without question," said the crown prince.

"I would like you to remain in a secret place for a while, until I come for you. In addition, I would like all of your ornaments and your valuable clothing as well."

"You may have them," said the crown prince.

Buddhivir then took the prince to his friend the businessman, who agreed to hide him and keep the matter secret.

Later that day, Buddhivir went into the forest and killed a deer. He dipped the prince's clothing and ornaments in the deer's blood. When he returned home, he showed his wife the bloody clothing and ornaments, saying, "Oh, my dear wife, a terrible thing has happened. By accident, when we were hunting, I killed the crown prince. There is no doubt that the king will kill me. I must go before him and seek my punishment."

"Oh, my husband, you must be surely grieving for the crown prince and eager for the king's punishment. But stay a while. Let me ask my father's advice."

"There is no need of that," Buddhivir moaned. "I am guilty and must be punished."

"But you did not do it deliberately. It was an accident. There is hope that the king will forgive you. You will have to have patience and let my father handle this. The king is very wise and my father a good counselor. Have patience."

Buddhivir's wife then picked up the crown prince's bloody clothing and ornaments and set off for her father's house. When she arrived, she showed him the bloody garments and told him all that had happened. Then she broke down crying, entreating her father to save her husband or she would kill herself.

Her father quickly took up the bloody garments and went before the king. The king, seeing the general looking so sad, asked him what the trouble was.

"Oh king, I am in a dilemma. Please help me find a way out." "Tell me everything," said the king.

"Oh king, my son-in-law was hunting a deer and accidentally killed a person of great stature. Now he wants to surrender himself to the law. He is ready to accept a sentence of death."

"I know that your son-in-law is honest, wise, humble, and brave and would not kill without reason. I trust him if he says it was an accident. It proves his greatness that he is willing to take his punishment. But tell me, whom did he kill?"

"Oh king, it was the crown prince. Here are your son's clothing and ornaments."

The king was shocked and immediately ordered his soldiers to bring Buddhivir before him. Buddhivir's wife stood by his side.

"Oh Buddhivir, what have you done?" cried the king. "How did you kill my son, who was the dearest in all the world to me? Tell me. You were appointed to guard him, but you killed him. How should I punish you?"

"Oh king, I would have killed myself on the spot, but I had to bring you the news. Now I am ready for any punishment. Please kill me, for I cannot live any longer with my grief."

"Have mercy, oh king!" cried Buddhivir's wife.

"Have mercy!" cried the general.

The king, wiping the tears from his cheeks, spoke softly, "Oh Buddhivir, I would not like to lose another son. I forgive you and accept you as my crown prince."

The king embraced Buddhivir, and all the courtiers exclaimed, "Long live the king! Long live the king!"

Buddhivir's wife called out, "Long live the king!"

The general shouted, "Long live the king!"

"Oh king, you are indeed great," said Buddhivir, "and you will be known far and wide as the wisest and kindest person in the world. Now if you would allow it, let me present you with a most precious gift."

The king sighed. "I have lost what is most precious. However, I do not wish to offend you, so I will accept what you offer."

"Oh king, let me go to my friend the businessman, and I will come back with your present." The king allowed Buddhivir to go to his friend. In no time, Buddhivir was back in the court, hauling a cart in which something lay hidden under a large cloth. "What is this?" asked the king.

Buddhivir uncovered the present, and the king stepped back in amazement. All of his courtiers gasped. The crown prince stood before them! The king rushed to embrace him.

Buddhivir said, "I am sorry, oh king, to have caused you such grief. I did this to test my grandfather's rules. I have now learned some truths about life and should like to return home. I told you I was a prince, but now I am king and must go home to rule my country."

"Oh noble King Buddhivir, you are like a son to me, so it is difficult to say good-bye. But I understand it is time for you to leave. Before you go, please share with us all you have learned."

Bhuddivir then repeated the words of his grandfather: Make friends with well-bred people. Marry a girl from a well-bred family. Work for a well-bred king.

All the courtiers were pleased with Buddhivir's words, and the king, the crown prince, the businessman, and the general all praised his wisdom. Then they said good-bye.

Buddhivir returned to his country, his beloved wife at his side. He ruled his people with wisdom, and they were happy under his reign. ❦

Tuhuro and the Bread-Bearing Tree

Once in a certain village lived a motherless child named Tuhuro. Though his father was kind to him, his stepmother was horribly cruel. She forced him to do all the work of the house but never gave him enough to eat. She made him live on the ground floor, among the goats and the chickens, while the rest of the family lived above.

Now the time came for *Dasain*, the biggest and gayest of all the festivals. The people of the village were busy preparing the most delicious feasts of the year. They served their children hearty meals of meat and fine rice.

But Tuhuro was treated no differently during this happy season. He gnawed only on dry bread made from the husks of corn. When his father asked his stepmother to give him some bread made of fine white rice flour, the woman only hurled a crust at the hungry boy. Tuhuro tried to catch the crust, but it rolled by him and out the door, down the path and toward the road. Finally he caught up with it and was just about to eat it, when he had an idea. "What if I plant this crust in the ground?" he thought. "Perhaps a tree will grow bearing bread on all of its branches. Then I need never go home and I will never again be hungry."

Pleased with his idea, Tuhuro ran to the outskirts of the village and dug a deep hole. He buried the crust of bread and after a time, a lovely tree grew up, bearing bread on all of its branches. Tuhuro was delighted and climbed up into the high branches of the tree. There he filled his stomach with delicious fresh bread, pleased to be far from his cruel stepmother.

After a time, an old giantess walking by smelled the boy high in the tree. Glancing up, she saw Tuhuro looking wonderfully plump. Her great mouth watered, and she tried to think of a way she could capture him and have him for supper.

Now the giantess knew she couldn't climb the tree, so she called up, "Dear little boy, I am an old woman who has been without food for many days. Can you spare me some bread? The gods will surely reward you."

The boy, taking pity on the old woman, plucked a loaf from the nearest branch and dropped it to the ground. The giantess pretended to try to catch it but instead let it fall into a heap of dung. "Oh dear," she whined. "Now see what has happened. The loaf is ruined. Won't you come down and hand me another?"

The kindhearted boy climbed down from the tree with another loaf in his hand. But when his feet touched the ground, the old woman grabbed him and stuffed him into her sack. Then quickly she made her way home.

Feeling thirsty along the way, she stopped and asked a farmer where she could find some water. The farmer pointed to a nearby stream, and the old woman put down her sack and went to have a drink.

The farmer, noticing something moving inside the sack, went to have a look. You can imagine his surprise when he opened the sack and out popped Tuhuro. The boy told him his story and asked for his help. The farmer agreed, and the two decided to trick the giantess by filling her sack with small boulders and stinging nettle plants.

When the old woman came back from the stream, she picked up her sack and ambled on, her load feeling heavier than before and stinging her back. She thought the boy must be pinching her. "I know how to deal with you, naughty boy," she scolded. "When my sharp teeth sink into your plump body, you will know why I have taken so much trouble with you."

When the giantess reached home it was dusk, and her daughter stood waiting in the doorway. "Here's a splendid feast for both of us," the giantess said, throwing the sack in a corner. "Start the water boiling, while I sharpen my teeth."

The obedient girl did as she was told, but when she opened the sack, all she could see were some sharp-edged rocks and a clump of stinging nettle plants. The old woman was puzzled, but she only said to her daughter, "Line the hearth with rocks, for tomorrow we will feast."

The next day the giantess went back to the bread-bearing tree and, in her sweetest voice, called up to the boy sitting high in its branches. "Have pity on a hungry old woman and bring me down some bread."

The boy, recognizing the woman, refused. Now the old woman tried harder.

"My eyesight is so poor. Yesterday I mistook you for a loaf of bread and tossed you in my sack. Today I am so hungry I would like only enough bread to fill my empty stomach." Tuhuro, taking pity on the old woman, came down from the tree, this time carrying two loaves of bread.

When his feet touched the ground, the old woman grabbed him and stuffed him into her sack, tying it tighter than before. She went directly home, not stopping for an instant. She greeted her daughter in the doorway, saying, "Kill and cook what is in this sack. I am going to the blacksmith's to sharpen my teeth."

The giantess left, and the obedient girl opened the sack. You can imagine her surprise when out leaped Tuhuro, looking so handsome and kind she could not bear to strike him.

Instead she led him to the back of the house where a swift horse was standing. Tuhuro jumped on the horse's back and, calling his thanks to the giantess' daughter, he rode off. When he reached the bread-bearing tree, Tuhuro climbed up into its branches, where he stayed for the rest of his days, in peace and contentment, his stomach always round and full. 🐦

Closing Comments

In Nepal, at the end of each storytelling a little verse is typically recited.

Garland of gold to the listener.
Garland of flowers to the teller.
May this tale go to heaven
and come down to be told again.

The following pages contain, in Nepalese script, the last tale presented here, in hopes that the beauty of the stories is enhanced by seeing the beauty of the written language.

टुहुरो र रोटी फल्ने रुख

एकादेशमा धेरै पहिले आमा नभएको एउटा टुहुरो बस्दथ्यो । उसको बुबा उसलाई धेरै माया गर्दथ्यो तर सौतेनी-आमा भने एकदमै निर्दयी थिइन् । तिनले उसलाई घरका धेरै काम लगाउँथिन् तर खान भने कहिल्यै पनि राम्ररी दिँदैन थिइन् । तिनले उसलाई छिंडीमा गाई-बस्तुसँगै सुत्न लगाउँथिन् र अरुलाई भने माथिल्लो तल्लामा सुताउँथिन् ।

दशैं आयो । गाउँमा सबैले मीठा-मीठा खाना बनाए र सबैले आफ्ना बाल-बच्चाहरुलाई मासु-भात खुवाए ।

तर टुहुरोको लागि भने केही फरक भएन । यत्रो ठूलो चाड आउँदा पनि भुसको रोटी खाएरै उसले चाड मनाउनु पर्‍यो । उसको बाबुले सौतेनी-आमालाई टुहुरोको लागि पनि एउटा चामलको रोटी छुट्याउनु भनेर अह्रायो । सौतेनी-आमा रिसले आगो भइन् र एउटा रोटीको डढेको माम्रा टुहुरोतिर हुत्याइ दिइन् ।

टुहुरोले त्यो माम्रालाई समात्न सकेन । त्यो गुडिएर ढोकाबाट बाहिर गयो । ऊ त्यसको पछि पछि गयो । तर माम्रा गुडिएर ओढालो लाग्यो । निक्कै तल बाटोमा पुगेपछि मात्र त्यो माम्रालाई उसले भेट्यो ।

उसले त्यो माम्रा खानै मात्र लागेको थियो कि, उसको मनमा एउटा बिचार आयो- "यो रोटीलाई रोपें भने कसो होला ? पक्कै पनि यसबाट बिरुवा उम्रने छ र हाँगाभरी रोटी फल्नेछ ।"

टुहुरो खुशी भयो । त्यसपछि गाउँ बाहिर गएर उसले खाल्डो खन्यो र त्यहाँ नै रोटीको माम्रा गाड्यो ।

केही समयपछि त्यहाँ एउटा कल्कलाउँदो बिरुवा उम्रियो र त्यसका हाँगाहरुमा रोटी फल्यो ।

टुहुरो अति नै खुशी भयो र रुखमा चड्यो । उसले रोटीहरु टिपेर पेटभरी खायो । अब उसलाई सौतेनी आमाको पीर भएन । ऊ सुखी भयो ।

धेरै समयपछि त्यतै भएर एउटी राक्षस्नी-बुढी हिंड्दै आइपुगी । त्यहाँ त्यसले त्यो टुहुरोको गन्ध पाई । त्यसले यताउती हेरी र माथितिर हेर्दा रोटी खाएर मोटो भएको टुहुरोलाई देखी ।

उसलाई देखनेबित्तिकै त्यस बुढीले राल काढी र अब यो केटोलाई कसरी खाने भनी उपाय सोच्न लागी ।

त्यो राक्षस्नी-बुढीलाई लाग्यो कि, ऊ त्यो रुखमा चढ्न सक्दिन । त्यसकारण त्यसले टीठलाग्दो पारामा भनी- "बाबु, म बुढी मान्छे धेरै दिनदेखि भोकै छु, मलाई पनि रोटी भारी देऊ न ! तिमीलाई धर्म हुन्छ ।"

बुढी देखेर टुहुरोलाई धेरै माया लाग्यो र एउटा रोटी टिपेर भूइँमा झारिदियो । राक्षस्नी-बुढीले पनि त्यो रोटी बीचैमा समात्न खोजेको जस्तो मात्र गरी र जानाजानी भूइँमा भएको गुहुमा खस्त दिई ।

राक्षस्नी-बुढीले भनी - "थुइक्क, हेर त, रोटी त खानै नहुने भयो । तलै ल्याइदेउ न बाबु ।"

त्यो दयालु टुहुरो एउटा रोटी लिएर तलै झ्यो । तर त्यो टुहुरोले भूइँमा खुट्टा राख्न पनि पाएको थिएन कि, राक्षस्नी-बुढीले उसलाई च्याप्पै समातेर बोरामा खाँदखुँद पारेर कोची । त्यसपछि छिटो छिटो गरी आफ्नो घरतिर लागी ।

बाटोमा राक्षस्नी-बुढीलाई तिर्खा लाग्यो र एउटा हलो जोत्दै गरेको किसानलाई पानी कहाँ पाइएला भनेर सोधी । उसले नजिकैको पानी आउने खोल्सा देखाइदियो । राक्षस्नी-बुढी भारी बिसाएर पानी खान गई ।

त्यो किसानले बोराको भारीमा केही चलमलाएको देख्यो । त्यसमा के रहेछ भनी बुझ्न उसले भारी खोलेर हेर्यो । भारीमा टुहुरोलाई देखेर ऊ चकित भयो ।

टुहुरोले किसानलाई सबै बेलीबिस्तार लायो र मलाई बचाउ भनेर मद्दत माग्यो । किसानले उसको कुरा मान्यो र दुबै मिलेर राक्षस्नी-बुढीलाई छक्याउन भारीमा ढुङ्गा र सिस्नो हालिदियो ।

राक्षस्नी-बुढी पानी खाइवरी फर्केर आई र आफ्नो भारी बोकी । त्यसलाई यो भारी पहिलेभन्दा गह्रुङ्गो लाग्यो र सिस्नोले पनि पोल्यो । त्यसले सोची कि, त्यो केटोले उसलाई चिमोट्दै छ ।

त्यसले भनी- "पख्लास्, तँ दुष्टलाई के गर्छु । मैले दाह्रा गाढेपछि थाहा पाउनेछस् कि, मैले किन यत्रो दुःख बेसाइरहेको छु ।"

घर पुग्दा साँझ परिसकेको थियो । राक्षस्नी-बुढीको छोरी आमालाई पिँढीमै पर्खेर बसिरहेकी थिई ।

भारी बिसाउँदै राक्षस्नी-बुढीले भनी- "ल आजलाई गज्जबको खाना ल्याएको छु । पानी उमाल्दै गर्नु ! म दाह्रा उध्याउन कामीकहाँ जान्छु ।"

आमाले अह्राए बमोजिम त्यो केटीले पानी उमाली र जब भारी खोलेर हेरी, त्यहाँ त्यसले ढुङ्गो र सिस्नोको मुठा मात्र देखी ।

राक्षस्नी-बुढी फर्केर आएपछि छक्क परी र छोरीलाई भनी - "ठीकै छ, यो ढुङ्गाले यहाँ चुलो बनाएर राख । हाम्रो भोजन भोली हुनेछ ।"

भोलीपल्ट राक्षस्नी-बुढी त्यही रोटीको रुख भएको ठाउँमा पुगी र रुखमा चढेर बसेको टुहुरोलाई मायालाग्दो स्वरमा भनी - "यो भोको बुढीलाई पनि रोटी ल्याई देउ न बाबु ।"

टुहुरोले त्यो राक्षस्नी-बुढीलाई चिन्यो र उसको कुरै सुनेन ।

राक्षस्नी-बुढीले अरु कोशिस गर्दै भनी - "म बुढीको आँखा नै कमजोर छ बाबु के गर्ने ? हिजो रोटी भनेर तिमीलाई पो बोरा भित्र कोचेछु । आज साह्रै भोकाएको छु । मलाई यहाँ नै पेटभरि खान पुग्ने रोटी भए पुग्छ । म भारी हाल्दिंन । लौन बाबु दया गर ।"

बुढी देखेर टुहुरोलाई दया लाग्यो र यसपल्ट झन दुइवटा रोटी लिएर तल झ्र्यो ।

तर राक्षस्नी-बुढीको चाला नै त्यही । टुहुरोले खुट्टा भूइँमा राख्नै पाएको थिएन कि, उसलाई गाँजीहाली र आफ्नो बोरामा कोचकाच पारेर हाली । यसपल्ट त अझ बलियो गरी बोराको मुख पनि बाँधी । त्यो कहींपनि रोकिइन र सिधै घर पुगेर मात्र भारी बिसाई ।

राक्षस्नी-बुढीले ढोकैमा पर्खिरहेकी छोरीलाई भनी - "लौ छोरी, यो बोरामा भएको शिकारलाई मार्नु र पकाएर राख्नु । म कामीकहाँ गएर दाह्रा उध्याएर आउँछु ।"

राक्षस्नी-बुढी गई । त्यसपछि छोरीले बोरा खोलेर हेरी । त्यहाँबाट टुहुरो निस्कियो । यस्तो राम्रो र दयालु ठीटो देखेर राक्षस्नी-बुढीको छोरीलाई दया लागेर आयो । त्यसले उसलाई मार्न सकिन । अझ उल्टै उसलाई घर पछाडी लगेर बायुपंखी घोडा दिई र भागी हाल भनी ।

टुहुरो तुरुन्तै घोडामा चढ्यो र राक्षस्नी-बुढीको छोरीलाई धन्यवाद दिँदै सुइंकुच्चा ठोक्यो ।

टुहुरो फेरि त्यही रुखमा पुग्यो र त्यसमाथि चढ्यो । ऊ त्यहाँबाट कहिल्यै झरेन । उसको पेट सधैं भरिलो र अघाएको हुन्थ्यो । त्यसरी ऊ सुखसंग बस्न लाग्यो ।

सुन्नेलाई सुनको माला,
भन्नेलाई फूलको माला,
यो कथा वैकुण्ठ जाला,
भन्ने वेलामा तुरुन्तै आइजाला ।

Glossary

atithi devo bhava—"the guest is like a visiting god"

baagh-chaal—game similar to Chinese checkers

badai—fireworks

bas paincha?—"Is there shelter for the night?"

bel—wood apple

boddhisatva—a holy man

Brahmin—a member of the highest order in the Hindu caste system

Cave of Halesi—a place of religious pilgrimage

chaitya—family shrine

chhang—beer

chiya—tea

chautara—a low stone wall

dai—elderly brother

dal baat tarkaari—classic Nepalese meal of lentils over rice with curried vegetables

Dasain—biggest Hindu festival, lasting 15 days in September and October

daura-suruwal—men's white Newar suit

dharma—holy deed

dharmsala—inn

dzo—animal which is a cross between a yak and cattle

gaine—wandering minstrels

ghee—butter

gompa—small monastery

hansia—sickle

jaand—a local beer made of either millet, rice, wheat, or maize

janai—holy thread worn by men of Brahmin or Chhetri castes upon reaching puberty

jhankri—witch doctor or traditional healer

jyotshi—fortune teller

Kaliyug—The Iron Age, a time of man's inhumanity to man. In this age, man eats meat and dairy products in great quantity and may even eat human flesh. Some believe that after all the human meat is eaten and there are no people left, the *Satyayuga*, the Age of Truth, will begin (Coburn, 41)

karma—good deeds and thoughts

Lake Phewa or *Phewatal*—the biggest and most beautiful of the five lakes in the Pokhara Valley

laligurans—rhododendron, the national flower of Nepal

lingum—male symbol

Lord Mahadeva—another name for Lord Shiva

Lord Paruhang—Lord Shiva, to the Kirati people of Nepal

Mahatma—Holy One

marcha—herbs that aid in fermentation

mit—male friends forever, almost a member of the family

mitini—best female friend

mohar—gold coin stamped with the royal sign

Mt. Halesi—in the foothills of the Himalayas of eastern Nepal

musli—a pestle used in grinding grain

Naga—serpent linked with obscure forces of the underworld which guards the treasures hidden in the womb of the earth and the springs which give it life

Namaste!—Greetings!

namlo—strap

narsinga—a long trumpet-like instrument

om mane padme um— Buddhist mantra: the jewel is in the lotus

panchayat—a traditional court attended by five elders of the community

pipal—banyan tree

puja—worship

Ram—Lord Rama, hero of the *Ramayana* and the seventh incarnation of Lord Vishnu

River Kamala—in eastern Nepal between the Mahabharat Range and the Siwalik Mountains

roti—pancakelike bread

rungi chungi topi—a colorfully striped cap

rupee—a small sum of money

sadhu—Hindu holy man

saint—holy man

Sagarmatha—Mt. Everest, "Roof of the World"

sanyasi—a holy man

sarangi—mournful twanging violin-like instrument

sari—Nepalese dress

stupa—a Buddhist shrine

tathastu—"let it be"

Teej—the Festival of Women

thankas—religious painting showing the life of Buddha

thirty-two good qualities—Hindus believe that the perfect person has all thirty-two good qualities, including kindness, patience, courage, and wisdom

tika— for worshippers, blessings of rice grains mixed with red liquid placed in the middle of the forehead representing the eye of the inner vision of wisdom

topi—traditional Nepalese hat

ukalo bokne namlo—tales told as a distraction while carrying heavy burdens on the trails of the mountains, also called "the strap to carry the uphill trail"

uttis—evergreen that grows primarily at the bottom of cliffs and where there have been landslides

yoni—female symbol

Bibliography

Antin, Parker, with Phyllis Wachob Weiss. *Himalayan Odyssey: The Perilous Trek to Western Nepal*. New York: Donald I. Fine, 1990.

Apte, Robert Z. *Three Kingdoms on the Roof of the World: Bhutan, Nepal, Ladakh*. Berkeley, CA: Parallax Press, 1990.

Armington, Stan. *Trekking in the Nepal Himalaya*. 6th ed. Berkeley, CA: Lonely Planet Publications, 1994.

Bernstein, Jeremy. *The Wildest Dreams of Kew*. New York: Simon & Schuster, 1970.

Bubriski, Kevin. *Portrait of Nepal*. San Francisco: Chronicle Books, 1993.

Burbank, Jon. *Cultures of the World: Nepal*. New York: Marshall Cavendish, 1991.

Cameron, Ian. *Mountains of the Gods*. New York: Facts on File Publications, 1984.

Choegyal, Lisa. *Insight Guides Nepal*. Boston: APA Publications/Houghton Mifflin, 1993.

Coburn, Broughton. *Nepali Aama, Portrait of a Nepalese Hill Woman*. Santa Barbara, CA: Ross-Erickson, 1982.

Eiselin, Max. *The Ascent of Dhauligiri*. London: Oxford University Press, 1961.

Eskelund, Karl. *The Forgotten Valley*. New York: Taplinger, 1960.

Facts on File: Weekly World News Digest. New York: Facts on File, 1990, 1994.

Fisher, James F. *Sherpas: Reflections on Change in Himalayan Nepal*. Berkeley: University of California Press, 1990.

Forbes, Ann Armbrecht. *Settlements of Hope: An Account of Tibetan Refugees in Nepal*. Cambridge, MA: Cultural Survival, 1989.

Furer-Haimendorf, Christoph von. *The Sherpas of Nepal, Buddhist Highlanders*. Berkeley: University of California Press, 1964.

Gibbons, Bob, and Bob Ashford. *The Himalayan Kingdoms, Nepal, Bhutan, Sikkim*. New York: Hippocrene, 1983.

Hagen, Tony. *Nepal*. Chicago: Rand-McNally, 1961.

Hansen, Eric. Photographs by Hugh Swift. *The Traveler: An American Odyssey in the Himalayas*. San Francisco: Sierra Club Books, 1993.

Hedrick, Basil C., and Anne K. Hedrick. *Historical and Cultural Dictionary of Nepal*. Metuchen, NJ: The Scarecrow Press, 1972.

Hillary, Sir Edmund. *Schoolhouse in the Clouds*. Garden City, NY: Doubleday, 1964.

Hillary, Sir Edmund, and Desmond Doig. *High in the Thin Cold Air*. Garden City, NY: Doubleday, 1962.

Hillary, Louise. *High Time*. New York: Dutton, 1974.

———. *A Yak for Christmas*. Garden City, NY: Doubleday, 1969.

Hosken, Fran P. *The Kathmandu Valley Towns*. New York: Weatherhill, 1974.

Hutt, Michael James, trans. and ed. *Himalayan Voices: An Introduction to Modern Nepali Literature*. Berkeley: University of California Press, 1991.

———, ed. *Nepal in the Nineties: Versions of the Past, Visions of the Future*. SOAS Studies on South Asia. New York: Oxford University Press, 1994.

Kelly, Thomas L., photographs. Text by Carroll Dunham. *The Hidden Himalayas*. New York: Abbeville Press, 1987.

Matthiessen, Peter. *The Snow Leopard*. New York: Viking, 1978.

Mumford, Stan Royal. *Himalayan Dialogue*. Madison: University of Wisconsin Press, 1982.

Murphy, Dervla. *The Waiting Land: A Spell in Nepal*. Woodstock, NY: The Overlook Press, 1987.

Norgay, Tenzing. *Tiger of the Snows*. New York: G. P. Putnam's Sons, 1955.

Pye-Smith, Charlie. *Travels in Nepal: The Sequestered Kingdom*. London: Penguin Books, 1990.

Raj, Prakash A. *Kathmandu and the Kingdom of Nepal*. Kathmandu: Naban Publications, 1993.

Reed, David. *Nepal: The Rough Guide*. 2nd edition. London: Rough Guides, 1993.

Samson, Karl. *Frommer's Comprehensive Travel Guide, Nepal*. New York: Prentice Hall Travel, 1993.

Savada, Andrea Matles, ed. Federal Research Division, Library of Congress. *Nepal and Bhutan: Country Studies*. DA Pam 550-35. Department of Army, 1993.

Scot, Barbara J. *The Violet Shyness of Their Eyes: Notes from Nepal*. Corvallis, OR: CALYX Books, 1993.

Singh, Madanjeet. *Himalayan Art*. Greenwich, CT: New York Graphic Society with UNESCO, 1968.

Taylor-Ide, Daniel. *Something Hidden Behind the Ranges: A Himalayan Quest*. San Francisco: Mercury House, 1995.

Valli, Eric. *Dolpo: Hidden Land of the Himalayas*. New York: Aperture Foundation, 1987.

Wheeler, Tony, and Richard Everist. *Lonely Planet, Nepal*. Australia: Lonely Planet, 1993.

Willison, Bert, and Shirley Bourke. *People Within a Landscape*. Seattle, WA: The Mountaineers; New Plymouth, New Zealand: with The Four Sherpa Trust, 1992.

For Children

Aung San Suu Kyi. *Let's Visit Nepal*. London: Burke, 1985.

Cherisey, Christine de. *Tsiza and the Caravans: My Village in Nepal*. Morristown, NJ: Silver Burdett, 1985.

Knowlton, Marylee, and Mark J. Sachner, eds. Photography by Hitomi Watanabe. *Children of the World: Nepal*. Milwaukee, WI: Gareth Stevens, 1987.

Lye, Keith. *Take a Trip to Nepal*. New York: Franklin Watts, 1988.

Margolies, Barbara A. *Kanu of Kathmandu: A Journey in Nepal*. New York: Four Winds Press, 1992.

Nepal in Pictures. Visual Geography Series. Minneapolis, MN: Lerner Publications, 1989.

Pitkanen, Matti A. *The Children of Nepal*. Minneapolis, MN: Carolrhoda, 1990.

Reynolds, Jan. *Himalaya*. Vanishing Culture Series. New York: Harcourt, 1991.

About the Authors

Kavita Ram Shrestha's science books for children, *Goddess of the Forest, Droplet,* and *The Story of Ants,* have won both national and UNICEF awards. Of his eight books for adults, one, *Confession,* has been translated into English. In 1987 Kavita Ram wrote and produced the first film for children in Nepal, a science adventure called *Rahashyamaya Gupha* (*A Mysterious Cave*). His most recent film, *Mukti Shangharsha,* about the democracy movement in Nepal, received an award at the 1994 Pyongyang International Film Festival in North Korea. The same year, he was named Man of the Year by the International Youth Forum in Nepal. In 1995 he was appointed chairman of the board of directors of Nepal Television.

Kavita Ram was born in the village of Okhaldhunga, at the foot of Mt. Everest in eastern Nepal. He received his B.A. from Tribhuvan University, Nepal, his M.A. in sociology from the University of Agra in India, and is currently working on his doctoral degree in medical sociology at Gorakhpur University in India. He lives in Kathmandu with his wife and three children.

Sarah Lamstein received her B.A. and M.A. in English literature from the University of Michigan and her M.L.S. from Simmons College. She was the school librarian at Milton Academy and the Roxbury Latin School, as well as library consultant at the Mather School in Boston. She has published poetry and children's stories in addition to her work as a puppeteer. On a family trip to Nepal, she was entranced by the country and drawn to explore its folk literature. Sarah lives with her husband in Newton, MA. She has three grown children. Her second book, *Annie's Sabbath,* will be published in 1997.